Find-a-Word
Book 4

Thi
diff
add
tra
itse
for

I
crossword
national newspapers, as well as being the author of the Beaver crossword books and *Find-a-Word* series. He is married, with two sons and two daughters, and lives beside a river in Norfolk where he enjoys sailing and birdwatching.

FIND -A- WORD 4

Pat Duncan

Beaver Books

First published in 1982 by
The Hamlyn Publishing Group Limited
London · New York · Sydney · Toronto
Astronaut House, Feltham, Middlesex, England
Paperback Division: Hamlyn Paperbacks
Banda House, Cambridge Grove
Hammersmith, London W6 0LE

ISBN 0 600 20297 6

Printed and bound in Great Britain by
Cox & Wyman Limited, Reading

Set in Univers

Foreword

Our fourth Find-a-Word book has a new look. It combines the familiar fun of Find-a-Word with the extra interest of a quiz book – so you have two kinds of entertainment in one.

This is how it works. With each diagram, you get a list of twenty-four general knowledge quiz questions instead of a list of words to find. The answer to each question is hidden somewhere in the diagram in the Find-a-Word way. The word or name you want may be read up or down, sideways or diagonally, backwards or forwards, but always in a straight line. Look at the diagram until you see the answer to the question, then put a line round it with your pen or pencil and go on to the next question.

Of course you won't know the answers to all the questions, unless you're Mastermind, Brain of Britain or Mr Knowall. But when you look at the diagram you'll soon find a word that must be the answer, or might be the answer, or sounds as if it ought to be the answer! If you aren't sure, have a go; don't be afraid to guess. And if you get stuck, try the puzzle the other way round: find a word or name in the diagram first and then see if there's a question to which it might be the answer. One warning, though: you may find extra words in the diagram which are not quiz answers!

Hunting through the diagram with a sharp eye, you'll soon find you know quite a bit more than you thought you did. In the end, though, you'll need to look up the answers, if only to confirm that you're right. But you can have extra enjoyment if you do this in two stages.

First, turn to the Answers in the back of the book and look at the quiz answers in the *Words* section. That will give you a list of twenty-four words and you can still have fun tracking these down in the diagram just as you would with a list of words in a Find-a-Word puzzle.

Then, when you've tried your Find-a-Word skill on the diagram you can turn to the *Diagrams* section of the Answers to check on any you might have missed.

Have fun with these!

Pat Duncan

1

1 Which Australian state is named after a Queen?
2 Which legendary Irish hero had a cave on the island of Staffa?
3 What is the first name of Scott, the author of the Waverley novels?
4 From which animal is perfume obtained?
5 Of which city is Schiphol the airport?
6 Which Italian statesman is remembered for his political cunning?
7 Who fought against the Roundheads?
8 What is the capital of Egypt?
9 Which country uses shekels for money?
10 Which seventeenth-century English composer wrote the opera *Dido and Aeneas*?
11 Which is the Sign of the Zodiac for late June and most of July?
12 Which town in West Yorkshire has the same name as a Canadian seaport?
13 Which Red Indian tribe sided with the Confederates in the American Civil War?
14 In which district of Northern Ireland does the town of Downpatrick stand?
15 Which great British physicist and chemist made important discoveries in electricity?
16 What is the word to indicate a broad and slow movement in music?
17 Which Roman statesman was called the Censor?
18 Which Cheshire town stands on the Manchester Ship Canal?
19 What is another name for a range of mountains?
20 What word describes the measurement across the widest part of a circle?
21 What roofing material comes from a quarry?
22 Matthew —— was the first man to swim the English Channel. Complete his name.
23 What is the device that provides nuclear power?
24 Which city is associated with Lady Godiva?

A	S	W	E	B	B	U	F	F	E	R
M	H	A	A	A	R	A	L	I	N	U
S	O	L	X	T	E	I	I	N	M	N
T	R	T	A	O	C	R	T	G	I	C
E	E	E	F	P	N	O	C	A	T	O
R	T	R	I	I	A	T	H	L	I	R
D	E	E	L	L	C	C	I	C	E	N
A	M	A	A	L	A	I	O	L	S	H
M	A	C	H	I	A	V	E	L	L	I
M	I	T	R	O	E	E	A	E	E	L
E	D	O	W	N	H	T	N	C	I	L
L	A	R	T	W	E	L	A	R	G	O
I	S	R	A	E	L	T	T	U	H	S
D	Y	A	D	A	R	A	F	P	T	S

2

1. Which great English portrait and landscape painter died in 1788?
2. What is the name of the country that was formerly known as Rhodesia?
3. Which ocean lies between Europe and America?
4. Which breed of dog is sometimes known as a German shepherd dog?
5. What is the great church in York called?
6. What is sometimes called balm of Gilead?
7. What is the word for a Spanish gentleman?
8. Which Canadian province lies between Ontario and Saskatchewan?
9. Who was the great enemy of the Christians during the third Crusade?
10. Of which country is Brussels the capital?
11. Who was Queen of the Netherlands during the last war?
12. Which is the biggest city in West Germany?
13. What is the sacred book of Islam?
14. Who loves Romeo?
15. Which American state has the smallest population?
16. Which precious stone is usually yellow?
17. Which English seaside resort is nearest to Beachy Head?
18. Which constellation contains the star Betelgeuse?
19. What is the capital of California?
20. What is the colour red called in heraldry?
21. Which famous school is near Windsor?
22. What money is used in Denmark?
23. Which is the chief city of the county of Avon?
24. What fibre is used for making sacks?

W	I	L	H	E	L	M	I	N	A	L
A	E	H	A	M	B	U	R	G	T	L
T	E	N	R	O	H	I	J	U	T	E
E	N	O	R	K	G	G	U	L	E	S
R	I	A	O	U	U	L	L	F	L	S
M	D	R	R	N	O	E	I	L	R	A
A	A	E	E	G	R	B	E	O	A	C
N	L	T	L	O	O	W	T	T	C	R
M	A	S	L	A	B	R	O	S	S	A
U	S	N	A	A	S	I	N	I	A	M
L	K	I	B	T	N	O	L	R	L	E
O	A	M	A	N	I	T	O	B	A	N
C	I	T	C	R	A	A	I	R	A	T
Z	A	P	O	T	G	R	N	C	M	O

3

1 Which great Carthaginian general led an army across the Alps?
2 Who turned back and became Lord Mayor of London?
3 What is the Eastern Mediterranean area called?
4 Which grass has a stem thick enough to make furniture?
5 What are gypsies sometimes called?
6 Where is Trent Bridge cricket ground?
7 Which British battleship gave its name to a whole class of warships?
8 Which Commonwealth country in West Africa is almost entirely surrounded by another state?
9 What part of a horse's harness is used to keep its head down?
10 What was the name of the giant David killed?
11 Which river flows through Burton and Gainsborough?
12 Graham —— is a famous modern novelist.
13 Which state of America is north of Wyoming?
14 What is the name for one of the people of southern Russia famous for horsemanship?
15 What is the name of the weaver in *A Midsummer Night's Dream*?
16 What is another name for the Friendly Islands?
17 Which species of ox is found in Tibet?
18 From which plant is a violet blue dye obtained?
19 What is another name for the love-apple?
20 What is the seaside resort between Portishead and Weston-super-Mare?
21 Which sweet is a paste filled with chopped almonds?
22 Which large white sea bird has black-tipped wings?
23 Which yellow-skinned fruit grows in the tropics?
24 Which American philanthropist provided libraries in many British towns?

C	A	Y	A	K	C	A	S	S	O	C
A	A	N	T	N	A	V	E	L	T	M
G	L	B	C	I	R	I	L	T	A	A
N	L	A	B	I	N	N	A	H	M	R
O	O	M	B	A	E	T	G	G	O	T
T	A	B	M	N	G	N	R	U	T	I
G	O	O	U	A	I	E	T	O	T	N
N	R	O	N	T	E	R	S	N	O	G
I	P	N	T	N	C	T	U	D	B	A
T	E	O	E	O	E	H	E	A	A	L
T	N	U	O	M	A	V	E	E	N	E
I	N	G	L	L	E	M	A	R	A	C
H	T	A	I	L	O	G	I	D	N	I
W	A	T	C	H	A	I	R	M	A	N

4

1 Name Britain's first woman Prime Minister.
2 Which musical instrument consists of a pair of bellows with vibrating reeds?
3 In which Shakespeare play does the central character have three daughters?
4 *Tales of Mystery and*——; can you complete the title of this book by Edgar Allan Poe?
5 What is the title of the Egyptian head of state?
6 Which marsh bird makes a booming sound?
7 What was the name of Henry VIII's first wife?
8 Which Greek sea-god had a dolphin's tail?
9 Which town stands where Eddleston Water runs into the Tweed?
10 Who is Harlequin's lover in pantomime?
11 Which city was the capital of Italy during the sixth and seventh centuries?
12 Who ruled England after William III?
13 In the Army which is the rank below Major?
14 Of which country is the the maple leaf the emblem?
15 In Greek mythology who was the goddess of good harvests?
16 Havana is the capital of which country?
17 Which French painter is regarded as the founder of impressionism?
18 Which New Zealand city is called by the Gaelic name for Edinburgh?
19 Which Roman emperor was noted for his magnificent games and buildings?
20 Which woodwind instrument of the oboe family has a lower range?
21 Which city on the River Douro is famous for the wine shipped from it?
22 On which Scottish island are buried Scots, Irish and Norwegian kings?
23 Name the largest South American water snake.
24 Which city stands on the River Ribble?

C	T	E	N	A	N	N	E	V	A	R
O	A	L	C	O	H	O	L	N	I	E
L	R	T	T	A	R	I	I	O	R	T
U	Q	R	H	P	N	T	M	R	N	E
M	U	I	A	E	R	A	A	E	S	M
B	I	T	T	E	R	N	D	M	E	E
I	N	O	C	B	L	I	O	A	L	D
N	O	N	H	L	S	G	N	C	T	D
E	O	T	E	E	M	A	N	E	T	U
C	S	T	R	S	C	M	A	I	I	N
T	S	P	S	O	T	I	J	O	K	E
A	A	A	N	E	P	O	A	N	S	D
R	B	D	A	U	R	O	R	A	K	I
Y	A	B	U	C	A	P	T	A	I	N

5

1 Which great composer became deaf?
2 The M1 starts from London; where does it end?
3 Which famous opera was written by Bizet?
4 Who was the youngest son of Jacob and Rachel?
5 Which plant with crimson or white flowers belongs to the buttercup family?
6 Who was the originator of vaccination?
Which Italian lake lies partly in Switzerland?
8 What is a country's representative in a foreign capital called?
9 Who was the sun-god worshipped by the Romans in Britain?
10 In which country is the yuan the unit of currency?
11 Which musical instrument can you suck as well as blow?
12 Joseph Mallord William were the Christian names of which great painter?
13 In which state is the most easterly point of the USA?
14 Which old county is now known as Gwent?
15 Which girl's name is the title of a novel by Jane Austen?
16 Which Belgian writer created the character Inspector Maigret?
17 Who was the rich man mentioned in the parable of Lazarus?
18 Which is the hardest of all minerals?
19 Pamplona is the chief town of which Spanish province?
20 In which Canadian city is a Stampede held every year?
21 Which British explorer died leading an expedition to the Antarctic?
22 Who was Moses' brother?
23 Who became Prime Minister in 1902?
24 Which town in Humberside is famous for its Minster?

S	U	N	I	M	A	J	N	E	B	E
R	L	C	O	O	E	N	I	A	M	Y
S	E	E	O	N	E	G	L	M	E	D
S	S	N	N	M	E	F	A	B	D	N
A	S	E	R	O	O	M	E	A	I	A
C	R	A	R	U	L	E	I	S	A	R
C	C	G	R	T	T	O	C	S	M	B
H	A	N	I	H	C	O	C	A	O	D
A	M	A	O	O	T	A	R	D	N	E
R	P	V	M	R	L	I	O	O	D	R
I	E	A	E	G	N	E	M	R	I	D
N	O	R	A	A	I	Y	E	R	V	N
E	N	R	T	N	A	N	R	D	E	U
T	Y	E	L	R	E	V	E	B	S	H

6

1 Who was Britain's leader during the last World War?
2 Which country has a nut named after it?
3 Johann Sebastian were the Christian names of which great composer?
4 Which character in fiction is associated with apes?
5 Where is Table Mountain?
6 What fruit comes from palm trees?
7 Which part of Ireland lies in the west of County Galway?
8 Who stuffs animals and birds?
9 Of which country is Dar es Salaam the capital?
10 A Babylonian temple shaped like a pyramid with steps – what is it called?
11 What do we call the method of calculating by symbols?
12 Which city is said to be the oldest in the world?
13 Who invented wireless-telegraphy?
14 Which sea lies between Sweden and the U.S.S.R.?
15 What is the county town of Berkshire?
16 Lambskin with curled wool is named after which town on the Caspian Sea?
17 What is the native dog of Australia?
18 Who is Scotland's most famous poet?
19 Which antiseptic can be obtained from seaweed?
20 Who was the Greek goddess of peace?
21 Which mountain range is found in North Africa?
22 Which Scottish leader was executed in London in 1305?
23 Which British colony gives its name to a sort of sailing rig?
24 On which river does York stand?

N	W	O	T	E	P	A	C	M	C	A
O	A	U	S	T	R	I	A	O	I	D
T	L	S	E	A	O	I	N	N	T	O
R	L	E	T	D	N	N	O	I	L	R
A	A	I	I	A	E	C	N	C	A	A
B	C	N	Z	M	R	A	H	A	B	B
B	E	N	A	A	O	U	S	N	A	I
I	A	R	M	S	R	N	G	I	L	Z
T	A	C	M	C	R	B	I	G	L	N
Y	A	O	H	U	N	T	E	T	I	A
B	T	I	B	S	D	I	N	G	O	Z
A	L	G	N	I	D	A	E	R	L	R
L	A	N	A	H	K	A	R	T	S	A
T	S	I	M	R	E	D	I	X	A	T

7

1. Who was the great Danish children's story writer?
2. Dakar is the capital of which West African country?
3. What is the highest human voice?
4. We use this man's name to mean refusing to work with someone – who was he?
5. Which big city stands on the Tyne?
6. What is a West Indian folk-song about current events called?
7. Which ancient city was the enemy of Rome?
8. What is the capital of Yugoslavia?
9. Which star is sometimes called the Dog Star?
10. Which ancient Greek is famous for his fables?
11. Which board game involves buying and selling property?
12. Who is the chief citizen of a town?
13. What would you sit in if you rode on an elephant?
14. Which university is associated with the colour light blue?
15. Which American city is famous for making cars?
16. Who wrote the Epistle to the Romans?
17. Which breed of dog is used for tracking fugitives?
18. Who was Laurel's comedy partner?
19. What was the nationality of the Kaiser?
20. Which British author wrote books about gypsy life?
21. What is another name for Odin, the Norse god?
22. What was the name of George IV's Queen?
23. What was an Indian prince called?
24. What is a glass cylinder used in laboratories called?

A	T	A	C	C	O	T	M	A	N	L
N	E	W	C	A	S	T	L	E	M	O
D	G	S	A	L	R	H	A	J	A	R
E	D	B	O	Y	C	O	T	T	Y	T
R	I	N	A	P	A	U	L	D	O	E
S	R	O	U	S	R	S	R	I	R	P
E	B	I	W	O	T	A	N	Y	N	T
N	M	N	S	P	H	N	N	L	T	E
E	A	U	U	H	A	D	W	O	H	S
G	C	M	I	Y	G	H	O	P	G	T
A	I	M	R	D	E	T	R	O	I	T
L	R	O	I	E	O	E	R	N	L	U
N	O	C	S	A	G	S	O	O	E	B
E	D	A	R	G	L	E	B	M	D	E

8

1 Name the land east of the Ural mountains.
2 In which school subject do you learn about substances?
3 Which great French writer invented the characters Gargantua and Pantagruel?
4 What is the Irish parliament called?
5 Which city in central Asia was once the capital of Tamerlane's empire?
6 What was a Barbary coast pirate called?
7 Which is the month for showers?
8 America's Birmingham is in which state?
9 Which creature sticks to ships' bottoms?
10 Which Mediterranean island is divided between Greek and Turkish communities?
11 Noel —— wrote plays and songs.
12 Which town in South Yorkshire is a railway and mining centre?
13 Who invented a process for making steel?
14 Who is the church dignitary in charge of a diocese?
15 What metal gives its name to a shade of blue?
16 What soft cheese comes from Normandy?
17 What is the name of the peninsula which includes Spain and Portugal?
18 In Greek mythology who helped Theseus escape from the labyrinth?
19 What shrub resembling the hawthorn bears red or orange berries?
20 Which Naval Captain wrote *The Children of the New Forest*?
21 Which region of Ghana was once a separate kingdom?
22 Who wrote the famous *Elegy Written in a Country Churchyard*?
23 What was the nationality of Mussolini?
24 In Greek mythology what was a sea-nymph called?

A	G	L	I	R	P	A	B	B	E	Y
S	U	E	E	K	O	R	E	H	C	R
I	I	T	N	A	H	S	A	P	E	T
A	L	H	R	T	S	R	N	T	I	S
L	D	E	M	E	I	S	S	E	N	I
E	I	A	M	A	B	A	L	A	C	M
B	E	E	D	A	E	M	N	R	C	E
A	R	N	C	N	R	A	E	S	O	H
R	E	E	O	A	I	R	C	M	B	C
N	N	T	W	L	A	K	Y	L	A	O
A	O	S	A	A	S	A	P	A	L	C
C	M	T	R	T	R	N	R	E	T	K
L	I	A	D	G	O	D	U	R	A	E
E	S	D	O	N	C	A	S	T	E	R

9

1 Who commanded the British Army at Waterloo?
2 Which country lies south of Romania?
3 What sort of sailing ship was square-rigged on the foremast only?
4 What is the capital of the German Federal Republic?
5 Which river unites with the Euphrates?
6 Which is the second largest city in Britain?
7 Who invented a burner for use in laboratories?
8 Which is the largest of the republics making up Yugoslavia?
9 Which Greek and Roman god was a model of manly beauty?
10 Which small bird, related to the pipit, can be grey, yellow or pied?
11 What is the Japanese name for Japan?
12 What was Churchill's first name?
13 Which Italian city is associated with violets?
14 Which long note of music is now no longer used?
15 In which American state is Chattanooga?
16 What was the name of the French royal family?
17 Who wrote the play on which the musical *My Fair Lady* was based?
18 Which great French river flows into the Bay of Biscay?
19 Who was the founder of Methodism?
20 Which is the main port of Iraq?
21 Who was Britain's main enemy during the last war?
22 What is the capital of South Australia?
23 Which musical instrument is sometimes called a fiddle?
24 Which is the chief city of Sicily?

B	A	R	S	A	B	U	N	S	E	N
R	I	D	S	E	R	B	I	A	O	A
E	A	R	E	O	I	R	I	P	B	R
V	G	W	M	L	G	R	P	O	L	R
E	I	A	A	I	A	I	L	L	E	O
E	N	O	T	G	N	I	L	L	E	W
S	N	Q	L	N	T	G	D	O	P	A
S	O	U	N	I	I	A	H	E	A	N
E	B	I	O	T	N	V	I	A	R	G
N	R	N	T	E	E	S	T	L	M	O
N	U	I	S	M	E	P	L	I	A	L
E	O	N	N	P	A	L	E	R	M	O
T	B	E	I	L	O	I	R	E	B	B
S	H	A	W	E	S	L	E	Y	A	R

10

1 Which animal's body is covered with small bony plates?
2 What was the name given to William I of England?
3 Who had a sword hung over his head?
4 Which is the biggest city in the state of Washington?
5 Who was the strong man who had his hair cut off by Delilah?
6 Part of Niagara Falls is in Canada – in which province?
7 Who is associated with Iseult in Celtic legend?
8 Which London club is associated with polo?
9 What is another name for mercury?
10 Which bird sings as it soars into the sky?
11 Which French writer, first name Jules, wrote *Around the World in Eighty Days*?
12 What is the old name for Thailand?
13 Lewis ——; can you name the author of *Alice in Wonderland*?
14 Which wading bird spears fish with its long bill?
15 Who was the greatest English playwright?
16 What is the capital of Jordan?
17 In snooker which ball scores highest?
18 After gold, which metal is most valuable in coins?
19 Which town in Derbyshire is eleven miles from Sheffield?
20 What is the name for a set of bells that plays tunes?
21 Which animal resembles the crocodile but has a broader head?
22 Which American Confederate general was called Stonewall?
23 In which city is the Eiffel Tower?
24 What was the first name of Presley the pop singer?

E	C	P	S	E	L	C	O	M	A	D
S	H	A	K	E	S	P	E	A	R	E
N	N	R	R	R	O	N	N	H	A	D
A	O	I	A	R	A	O	R	G	I	L
M	L	S	P	O	O	L	E	N	L	E
M	A	H	M	T	E	L	V	I	S	I
A	A	R	M	A	D	I	L	L	O	F
N	R	I	T	G	S	R	I	R	O	R
O	K	M	S	I	E	A	S	U	I	E
S	I	P	B	L	A	C	K	H	R	T
K	T	L	G	L	T	N	C	E	A	S
C	E	G	N	A	T	S	I	R	T	E
A	U	E	K	A	L	B	U	O	N	H
J	U	R	O	R	E	U	Q	N	O	C

11

1 Which Queen of Egypt is associated with Antony?
2 Which is the largest living bird?
3 Which canal joins the Atlantic to the Pacific?
4 Who was the most famous eighteenth-century Englishman associated with India?
5 Which is the Government minister in charge of the Exchequer?
6 What was the sacred beetle of ancient Egypt?
7 Which King of England succeeded Henry I?
8 What is the name of the dangerous sands in the Straits of Dover?
9 Who was the next Labour Prime Minister after Attlee?
10 Segovia became famous for playing which musical instrument?
11 Which part of France is famous for sparkling wine?
12 What is the capital of Vietnam?
13 Which plant of the lily family do people eat?
14 What was the Spanish fleet called which set out to attack England in 1588?
15 What is the old form of chanting used in some churches called?
16 Which town in North Yorkshire, apart from York, has a cathedral?
17 Which saint's day is on February 14?
18 Which great film comedian was famous for his cane and big boots?
19 Lammas is the first day of which month?
20 On which river does Windsor stand?
21 Which British Prime Minister declared war on Hitler?
22 Which city in Massachusetts has the same name as a town in Lincolnshire?
23 Who was Abel's brother?
24 Of which country is Burgundy a part?

N	O	L	Y	N	O	T	S	O	B	E
I	E	E	N	I	T	N	E	L	A	V
A	G	H	E	R	O	S	I	L	R	E
L	O	C	P	S	A	N	P	A	A	R
R	O	L	L	E	C	N	A	H	C	I
E	D	I	A	E	T	A	N	H	S	S
B	W	V	I	E	O	S	A	E	L	K
M	I	E	N	G	A	P	M	A	H	C
A	N	O	S	U	L	A	A	R	C	O
H	N	S	O	I	H	R	R	T	I	T
C	O	U	N	T	M	A	Q	U	R	N
O	P	G	G	A	U	G	U	S	T	A
M	I	R	D	R	S	U	I	S	S	U
F	R	A	N	C	E	S	S	U	O	Q

12

1 Who wrote the famous *Messiah* oratorio?
2 There's a song about a fair at which North Yorkshire seaside town?
3 Who invaded Britain with his brother Horsa and became King of Kent?
4 What does the Lord Chancellor sit on in the House of Lords?
5 Who wrote a famous Life of Doctor Johnson?
6 Ermine is the winter coat of which animal?
7 What was an officer called who commanded a hundred Roman soldiers?
8 What symbol of royal authority is held at a coronation?
9 Which islands in the Atlantic belong to Portugal?
10 What is a letter from an Apostle called?
11 Which famous outlaw was called 'the Wake'?
12 What is the name for the mouths of the Nile?
13 To which royal house did Henry VIII belong?
14 What is a sardine called when it is fully grown?
15 What is another name for a Nonconformist?
16 Which member of the weasel family eats fish?
17 *The Thirty-Nine Steps* and other adventure stories were written by John ——.
18 Which nut tree has pink flowers?
19 He was called The Venerable and was a historian; who was he?
20 Which fine white linen originally came from northern France?
21 What is a light-coloured crested Australian parrot called?
22 Which tree's twigs are used in basket-making?
23 Who composed a number of Hungarian Rhapsodies?
24 What is a curved cavalry sword called?

A	Z	O	R	E	S	O	P	M	O	C
T	H	I	S	T	R	T	U	D	O	R
L	C	E	P	I	S	T	L	E	T	E
E	L	C	R	I	E	E	P	E	A	T
D	N	E	G	E	L	R	I	E	K	N
N	R	N	W	R	W	C	T	D	C	E
A	E	T	O	S	E	A	H	I	O	S
H	G	U	O	R	O	B	R	A	C	S
C	A	R	L	T	O	B	E	D	R	I
U	L	I	S	N	M	A	N	E	T	D
B	I	O	A	A	D	N	O	M	L	A
A	S	N	C	N	B	E	D	E	L	L
N	Z	I	K	E	R	R	Y	T	A	S
A	T	C	Y	T	I	V	E	R	B	O

13

1 Which Italian patriot and liberator was famous for his red shirt?
2 Which island is famous for cake and wine?
3 Which Spanish king ruled jointly with Queen Isabella?
4 Where did Churchill and Roosevelt meet in North Africa during the last war?
5 —— *Rudge*; can you complete the title of a book by Dickens?
6 Who is famous for his theory of relativity?
7 What was ugly in a story by Hans Andersen?
8 What fizzy drink came to us from Persia?
9 Who was famous for his escapes?
10 What is the currency unit in Italy?
11 Which English king was called the Unready?
12 What is the Christian name of Princess Anne's husband?
13 Which country lies north and east of Lebanon?
14 What is the name for a wide moustache with curved ends?
15 *The Flying* ——; can you complete the name of the ghost ship of legend?
16 The rivers Trent and Ouse combine to form which estuary?
17 Who were the priests of the ancient Britons?
18 Which town in Northamptonshire has the nearest railway station to Corby?
19 Which French river was the scene of a great battle in September 1914?
20 What was Nebuchadnezzar's capital city?
21 'I remember, I remember, the house where I was born'. Which poet wrote these words?
22 Which instrument do you play by blowing across a hole in its side?
23 A famous Queen of France was —— Antoinette; what was her first name?
24 Name a frame used for calculating.

N	R	A	B	E	L	D	N	A	H	G
A	S	C	S	T	T	N	I	R	O	N
M	Q	N	Y	H	O	U	D	I	N	I
H	U	A	R	E	E	O	L	A	E	R
C	A	L	I	L	I	R	A	F	Y	E
T	R	B	A	R	N	A	B	Y	F	T
U	E	A	M	E	S	E	I	E	A	T
D	B	S	A	D	T	L	R	B	T	E
S	M	A	R	I	E	D	A	M	H	K
D	U	C	K	L	I	N	G	O	E	U
I	H	C	N	N	N	I	E	D	R	L
U	O	I	A	M	A	R	N	E	M	F
R	O	N	V	B	A	B	Y	L	O	N
D	D	T	E	E	A	S	T	O	N	E

1 What sort of school combines secondary modern and grammar?
2 Which city is associated with Beau Nash?
3 What equals 24 grains?
4 What is the capital of Greece?
5 Which animal of the cat family has spots?
6 Which seaside resort was made famous by the Prince Regent?
7 In which Indian city was a British garrison relieved by Sir Colin Campbell's forces after a long siege?
8 Which river joins the Thames at Reading?
9 Who works at a telephone switchboard?
10 A famous hospital at Smithfield, in London, is named after which saint?
11 Which is the lowest pass over the Alps, linking Germany and Italy?
12 What is the capital of Albania?
13 Which famous girls' school is near Brighton?
14 What is a dish of large prawns called?
15 Which seaside resort is nearest to the North Foreland?
16 What was a provincial governor called in ancient Persia?
17 Who takes care of your teeth?
18 Which South American river fish will attack people?
19 What is a doctor's written order called?
20 What is the capital of Morocco?
21 Which famous architect planned Regent Street in London and designed the Brighton Pavilion?
22 Which port lies at the Atlantic end of the Panama Canal?
23 Which is the most southerly state on the western side of India?
24 What is the stretch of water inside an atoll?

T	H	G	I	E	W	Y	N	N	E	P
O	T	O	Y	K	E	R	A	L	A	R
L	A	P	R	W	V	I	S	O	R	E
I	B	E	O	M	I	R	H	O	L	S
P	A	R	T	A	S	A	E	S	Y	C
M	R	A	I	R	N	D	N	K	N	R
A	T	T	R	G	E	E	K	B	O	I
C	H	O	A	A	H	N	A	R	I	P
S	O	R	N	T	E	T	N	E	S	T
C	L	L	A	E	R	I	O	N	S	I
H	O	A	O	N	P	S	O	N	I	O
O	M	N	T	N	M	T	G	E	M	N
O	E	D	L	E	O	P	A	R	D	U
L	W	O	N	K	C	U	L	G	A	S

15

1. The waltzes of Strauss are associated with which city?
2. Which flightless bird is found in the Antarctic region?
3. Chamois, gazelle and gnu are varieties of which animal?
4. Which Celtic hero led the resistance to the Roman invaders in AD 48–51?
5. Which silk fabric is named after a province of China?
6. What was Nelson's first name?
7. What is the United States parliament called?
8. Which planet was discovered in 1781?
9. What is the capital of Ghana?
10. Enrico —— was a great operatic tenor; can you supply the missing name?
11. Which great mountain in the Alps is otherwise known as Mont Cervin?
12. What is the double-flowering variety of the clove pink called?
13. What weapon is used to kill whales?
14. What are the grassy, treeless plains of Russia called?
15. What is the architectural style of most English cathedrals?
16. Which American furry animal has a ringed tail?
17. What is the capital of Norway?
18. What is the wife of an earl called?
19. In which area of France is Marseilles?
20. Which member of the cat family suggests very little weight?
21. Which great Protestant theologian is associated with the city of Geneva?
22. Which is the county town of Somerset?
23. What is the word for a wide or complete view?
24. Which is the highest of the nine orders of angels?

C	A	R	A	C	T	A	C	U	S	T
O	O	N	N	I	U	G	N	E	P	S
N	U	L	I	M	B	O	P	R	A	A
G	E	N	E	V	A	O	O	L	M	N
R	N	L	C	I	L	V	T	A	O	Y
E	A	U	Y	E	E	A	R	O	I	N
S	S	E	T	N	U	O	C	S	T	O
S	T	N	C	N	N	C	E	C	A	I
U	A	E	T	A	A	R	I	A	R	T
N	O	O	P	R	A	H	A	M	O	A
A	N	P	U	P	T	A	S	P	H	N
R	U	S	H	O	E	H	O	H	S	R
U	O	N	G	I	O	S	L	O	U	A
M	A	T	T	E	R	H	O	R	N	C

16

1 The buildings of Parliament are part of the Palace of which place?
2 Which drooping white flower appears in early spring?
3 Innsbruck is the capital of which part of Austria?
4 Who is the patron saint of Ireland?
5 Name the largest island belonging to Denmark.
6 Which German composer is associated with Romanticism?
7 Which seaside resort lies between Littlehampton and Shoreham?
8 Which tool is used for digging by hand in the garden?
9 Which bird has splendid blue and green tail feathers?
10 What is often nailed over a door to bring luck?
11 What happens when the moon comes between the sun and the earth?
12 Which American state is north of California?
13 What was George Stephenson's most famous locomotive called?
14 Which duck gives us down for bed covers?
15 Which Greek mountain was the seat of Apollo and the Muses?
16 In Shakespeare's *Hamlet* what is the name of his mother, the Queen?
17 On which river does Cologne stand?
18 What do deer have on their heads?
19 Which planet has rings round it?
20 What unit of the Army does a Colonel command?
21 In which county of Ireland does Blarney Castle stand?
22 Who became Poet Laureate after Southey?
23 Which chain of mountains is sometimes called the backbone of England?
24 What is the male rabbit called?

D	R	A	P	E	R	P	B	U	C	K
T	H	E	V	E	R	A	R	D	O	C
E	I	T	E	R	N	R	E	N	H	O
K	N	A	R	F	L	N	D	A	O	C
C	E	N	I	O	E	A	I	L	R	A
O	R	E	T	A	W	S	E	N	S	E
R	E	S	Y	A	O	S	R	E	E	P
K	G	E	R	T	R	U	D	E	S	O
C	I	C	O	E	T	S	S	R	H	R
I	M	A	L	A	H	P	U	G	O	D
R	E	T	S	N	I	M	T	S	E	W
T	N	S	I	L	N	O	G	E	R	O
A	T	U	C	I	G	A	R	T	I	N
P	R	E	N	N	A	M	U	H	C	S

17

1 What is the sea between Europe and Africa?
2 What is a Himalayan mountain guide called?
3 Which Scottish engineer is famous for his work on steam power?
4 Which famous street is also the name of a Cambridge college?
5 Which poet wrote *A Shropshire Lad*?
6 Which Poet Laureate went to sea as a boy?
7 What is the thick treacle that is drained from sugar?
8 Who is the Prophet of Islam?
9 What instrument enables us to see distant objects?
10 Which French revolutionary leader was called 'the sea-green Incorruptible'?
11 Which English city is also the name of a breed of cattle?
12 Which bird symbolises peace?
13 What is the capital of Canada?
14 What is the name of the lake in Hyde Park, London?
15 Which Bible person was hairy?
16 What is the cold, dry north-west wind that blows in southern France?
17 What is a song sung outside a lady's window?
18 From which animal do we get wool?
19 Which tiny organism can carry disease?
20 Which Somerset seaside town is nearest to Exmoor?
21 What is another name for allspice?
22 Which opera by Puccini was first performed in 1900?
23 What is the name of the large forest in Sussex?
24 What is the name of the great desert region of China?

E	L	B	M	U	M	H	M	S	O	T
R	N	L	I	I	I	P	E	E	H	S
R	A	I	S	I	N	R	D	P	A	E
E	S	A	T	G	E	U	I	O	N	G
I	M	T	R	N	H	M	T	C	N	G
P	A	E	A	I	E	T	E	S	A	U
S	S	D	L	N	A	P	R	E	H	S
E	E	R	T	W	D	E	R	L	O	E
B	F	O	A	O	G	I	A	E	U	S
O	I	F	V	D	S	H	N	T	S	S
R	E	E	E	H	E	C	E	G	M	A
C	L	R	R	S	L	O	A	O	A	L
I	D	E	N	A	I	N	N	B	N	O
M	O	H	A	M	M	E	D	I	U	M

18

1 Florence —— was famous for her nursing; can you supply her name?
2 Which great seaport is in Hampshire?
3 Who is regarded as the father of railways?
4 Who looks after a child instead of parents?
5 What is the name of Shakespeare's play about a Prince of Denmark?
6 Which animal is called the king of beasts?
7 Which musical instrument is shaped like a cauldron?
8 What is meat dried in the Red Indian way called?
9 What is the name for someone who tries to climb high peaks?
10 What name is applied to a dance or a dot?
11 What is the extra sail used when a yacht has the wind behind it?
12 What is another name for the Devil?
13 Which large forest tree has smooth grey bark and edible nuts?
14 What is the Eskimo seal-skin canoe called?
15 What is a pickle with mustard and spices called?
16 What is the capital of Nepal?
17 What was the name of the ship commanded by Captain Bligh in which a mutiny took place?
18 Which flightless bird, once found in Mauritius, is now extinct?
19 What is the word for a window that sticks out?
20 What is the nearest Norwegian port to Aberdeen?
21 In Greek mythology who was visited by Zeus in the form of a swan?
22 What winding device is turned by means of bars?
23 On which river estuary does Buenos Aires stand?
24 Which name is associated with two American states and the Black Hills?

R	E	E	N	I	A	T	N	U	O	M
E	N	B	O	U	N	T	Y	O	U	B
A	P	E	T	D	O	O	U	R	A	N
R	A	E	P	N	I	R	D	O	D	O
E	L	C	M	A	L	E	I	U	E	S
G	L	H	A	M	L	E	T	E	L	N
N	I	G	H	T	I	N	G	A	L	E
A	D	I	T	A	L	C	U	M	L	H
V	A	E	U	K	A	Y	A	K	E	P
A	K	L	O	P	C	C	R	N	A	E
T	O	O	S	R	C	L	D	T	K	T
S	T	T	R	A	I	E	I	I	R	S
S	A	T	A	N	P	O	A	R	A	B
N	O	R	E	K	A	N	N	I	P	S

19

1 Which British general won the battle of El Alamein in the last war?
2 Which of the Great Lakes of America is connected to Lake Michigan?
3 Which songbird is named after the islands in which it is found?
4 Which variety of grape has a musky smell?
5 What was the name of three sisters who all became famous writers?
6 What is a choral work intended for concert performance called?
7 What is the name of the skirt-like garment worn by men and women in Malaysia?
8 Which religious sect is based in Salt Lake City?
9 Which game is played in Commonwealth countries but not in the USA?
10 What is a Naval escort vessel called?
11 There's a song about marching through which American state?
12 Which winds bring heavy rain in India?
13 Which African country has borders with Nigeria, Chad and Gabon?
14 What is the shell of the crab or tortoise called?
15 What is the large maple tree called?
16 City and United are football teams in which city?
17 What is the optical illusion sometimes seen in the desert?
18 Where would you go to see a film?
19 What is the most southerly holiday resort in the Isle of Wight?
20 What is the name of the Dutch royal house?
21 Where did Nebuchadnezzar have Shadrach, Meshach and Abednego thrown?
22 William the Conqueror's invasion of Britain is known as what conquest?
23 What is found in the hollow parts of bones?
24 What entertainment takes place in a ring?

A	M	E	N	I	C	E	E	S	L	R
R	O	O	M	U	S	C	A	T	E	L
E	N	S	I	A	A	A	I	T	A	A
T	E	U	R	P	R	N	U	S	H	T
S	Y	C	A	M	O	R	E	I	U	E
E	R	R	G	O	N	U	O	H	R	M
H	A	I	E	R	G	F	B	W	O	A
C	N	C	A	M	E	R	O	O	N	G
N	A	K	T	O	O	I	A	E	T	G
A	C	E	A	N	R	G	R	P	N	O
M	D	T	T	S	G	A	T	A	E	T
R	A	E	N	O	I	T	N	N	V	H
O	C	L	A	O	A	E	L	G	O	A
N	E	L	C	N	P	H	T	A	E	M

20

1 Which British Queen ruled the Iceni and fought the Romans?
2 What is a gathering of witches called?
3 Where is the chief cathedral of the Church of England?
4 What was the name of the first space satellite?
5 Name the hat worn by Roman Catholic priests.
6 What is the capital of Denmark?
7 Who wrote the music of *Land of Hope and Glory*?
8 In which province of South Africa is Durban?
9 A famous fictional courtroom lawyer is —— Mason; what is his first name?
10 Which great Spanish painter painted a series of pictures *The Disasters of War*?
11 Which mountain range includes Mount Everest?
12 Where were the Olympic Games held in 1972?
13 What is an apple of the Cox's Orange variety called?
14 In Greek mythology who let all the human ills out of her box?
15 What is a piebald horse called in America?
16 What is a small, two-masted, fore-and-aft rigged sailing vessel called?
17 Which saint's day is November 11?
18 Which cotton cloth got its name from a town in India?
19 Who became Prime Minister of Britain at the age of 24?
20 Which fruit is coloured orange and of the plum family?
21 Which bird has a short hooked beak and a crest?
22 Of which former Ulster county was Omagh the county town?
23 Who invented a miner's safety lamp?
24 Which fabulous monster resembled a bird with a dragon's tail?

C	A	S	K	E	T	C	H	T	G	H
A	Y	O	C	I	L	A	C	O	O	P
M	A	R	T	I	N	H	I	R	Y	O
P	I	T	T	L	E	T	N	R	A	P
E	C	N	T	N	D	O	U	A	I	L
C	S	O	O	E	E	B	M	P	I	A
I	A	R	P	A	R	V	P	R	S	R
R	Y	R	R	E	P	I	O	I	R	C
T	A	V	T	C	N	I	B	C	A	H
A	L	N	A	I	R	H	N	O	E	E
K	A	N	T	D	E	O	A	T	L	R
C	M	R	A	A	A	R	T	G	O	S
O	I	A	R	O	D	N	A	P	E	U
C	H	A	M	B	E	R	L	A	I	N

21

1 Who was the author of *The Pickwick Papers* and *Oliver Twist*?
2 Which bird is traditionally associated with babies?
3 Where were the 1980 Olympic Games held?
4 Which great German composer died in 1897?
5 Who is to be found under the spreading chestnut tree in Longfellow's poem?
6 Which is the largest city in Canada?
7 Who wrote the play *The Importance of Being Earnest?*
8 What is the popular name for Chelsea football team?
9 What was Mrs Siddons' profession?
10 A famous book by Alexander Dumas is called *The Three* ——; what were they?
11 Which chess piece is also the name of a bird?
12 Which book of the Bible is associated with King David?
13 Which bird is the subject of a poem by Shelley?
14 In which American state does the River Mississippi rise?
15 Which tree is a symbol of mourning?
16 What colour is a carnation?
17 What is the lowest point, opposite to the zenith?
18 In Greek mythology who went down to Hades to bring back his wife Eurydice?
19 Which is the biggest city in the world?
20 Which football team plays in claret shirts with blue sleeves?
21 What is a festive gathering of Australian aborigines called?
22 Nairobi is the capital of which country?
23 Which ancient Greek city-state is associated with simplicity?
24 Which is the largest island in the Firth of Clyde?

N	A	T	R	A	P	S	A	L	M	S
P	R	E	I	M	E	R	P	H	N	S
E	A	H	D	B	N	L	I	C	A	M
R	M	W	A	L	S	D	T	O	R	H
C	O	U	N	A	I	T	I	R	R	A
Y	M	O	S	C	O	W	R	R	A	R
P	I	N	K	K	N	E	K	O	R	B
R	N	E	Y	S	E	S	S	B	T	I
E	N	O	L	M	R	T	U	O	A	N
S	E	P	A	I	S	H	E	R	R	Y
S	S	E	R	T	C	A	H	E	A	R
C	O	O	K	H	A	M	P	E	R	A
O	T	N	O	R	O	T	R	I	A	S
T	A	Y	N	E	K	R	O	T	S	T

22

1 Mark Twain wrote *The Adventures of —— Finn*; what was the character's first name?
2 Which Government body is formed by the most important ministers?
3 Who was Richard Coeur de Lion's Queen?
4 Which famous horse race is run at Epsom in June?
5 Where did the first passenger railway start . . .?
6 . . . and where did it finish?
7 Who gave his customers no choice?
8 In which city would you expect to see gondolas?
9 What is the surname of pretty little Polly of Paddington Green?
10 Who acts instead of a King?
11 On a ship what is the right-hand side called?
12 In Shakespeare's play what is the name of the Merchant of Venice?
13 What name is given to the battle in which William the Conqueror defeated Harold?
14 What is a helicopter sometimes called?
15 Whom did Leander swim the Hellespont to visit?
16 Which fish's name is also a measure of 5½ yards?
17 From which plant are cigarettes made?
18 Which country is shaped like a boot?
19 What is an Eskimo's snow house called?
20 What is the fashionable part of Central London called?
21 What instrument is used in the Army for summoning troops?
22 On which river does the city of Newcastle stand?
23 Which ancient city in Syria was called Queen of the East?
24 Which Moroccan port is nearest to Europe?

H	O	B	S	O	N	A	T	A	E	H
T	A	E	R	G	N	I	L	L	A	C
V	N	R	T	A	N	G	I	E	R	R
E	E	E	N	O	M	I	S	S	E	E
S	L	N	G	M	B	D	T	E	O	P
T	A	G	I	E	A	A	O	S	E	P
R	G	A	U	C	R	R	C	R	A	O
Y	R	R	E	B	E	L	K	C	U	H
B	L	I	O	H	E	I	T	A	O	C
R	R	A	E	I	N	N	O	B	O	O
E	R	F	T	S	I	G	N	I	C	I
D	A	Y	K	I	T	T	E	N	E	T
T	N	A	I	G	L	O	O	E	A	N
E	L	M	O	O	I	N	O	T	N	A

23

1 Which tree resembling the beech has hard, tough wood?
2 What is another name for Scotland?
3 Who was Lord Protector of England after the Civil War?
4 Which country owned the Shetland Islands?
5 What is a figure with many sides called?
6 Which girl's name is associated with an apple dish?
7 Which weapon moves through the water to sink an enemy ship?
8 What is another name for the adder?
9 What sort of shoe has an open top?
10 Which climbing shrub often has pale yellow flowers?
11 Which country is Britain's oldest ally?
12 What title did Queen Victoria assume in relation to India?
13 From which Italian port did Christopher Columbus come?
14 Which tree provides food for dessert and very fine wood for cabinet-making?
15 Which wind instrument has a single reed and a range like a violin's?
16 Which Australian animal is like a small bear?
17 Which is the highest peak in the hills between England and Scotland?
18 Which water bird has a white patch on the forehead?
19 Who is the eldest of King Lear's daughters?
20 Which game bird is related to the snipe?
21 On which river does Sunderland stand?
22 Which tree is sometimes called the locust-tree?
23 Where did Masefield's Quinquireme of Nineveh come from?
24 What was the name of the Bruce who became King of Scotland?

C	R	E	N	I	M	S	A	J	N	P
L	H	T	B	D	S	A	N	D	A	L
A	T	A	C	E	L	L	N	R	I	A
R	N	L	R	A	R	A	A	G	N	C
I	O	P	O	L	Y	G	O	N	O	K
N	M	K	M	A	O	U	J	N	D	E
E	D	A	W	N	S	T	R	E	E	T
T	T	R	E	B	O	R	T	M	L	G
U	O	R	L	B	N	O	T	E	A	H
N	I	R	L	R	N	P	B	S	C	A
L	V	I	P	E	R	R	O	R	A	N
A	E	H	T	E	E	T	O	O	C	A
W	H	P	O	N	D	L	O	H	I	O
K	C	O	C	D	O	O	W	E	A	R

24

1 Who likes to wallow in glorious mud?
2 Which town in Cambridgeshire was once the county town of a separate county?
3 Which lively southern Italian dance was once thought to cure dancing mania?
4 Who specialises in eye diseases?
5 What land of very small people did Gulliver discover?
6 What is the Chinese ceremony of touching the ground with one's forehead called?
7 Which people built the Pyramids?
8 Which part of East Kent was formerly separated from the mainland?
9 Who is the Roman equivalent of the Greek god Eros?
10 Which great French writer wrote the social satire *Candide*?
11 Which form of herring is associated with Yarmouth?
12 In Shakespeare's *Twelfth Night* who has Malvolio as a steward?
13 What poison was given to Socrates when he was sentenced to death?
14 Which ape is like the gorilla but smaller?
15 Who was David's great friend?
16 In Shakespeare's *The Merchant of Venice* who is Shylock's daughter?
17 Which card game can you play by yourself?
18 Which cross-bred dog like a greyhound is used for racing?
19 What sort of cheese is round with a red rind?
20 Which old kingdom now forms central Spain?
21 Who was goddess of the moon and hunting?
22 The book of which prophet follows Lamentations in the Bible?
23 Who was the wife of Isaac?
24 What is a warship's small motorboat called?

T	I	O	R	T	E	D	S	L	I	K
N	O	I	N	U	I	E	O	E	A	O
E	G	N	O	P	S	C	U	I	C	R
L	S	V	U	I	U	N	T	K	C	E
I	K	C	O	L	M	E	H	E	E	A
T	O	N	I	L	A	I	U	Z	B	L
S	W	S	A	I	T	T	N	E	E	L
A	T	E	B	L	O	A	T	E	R	E
C	O	L	T	E	P	P	I	H	W	T
I	W	L	D	M	O	I	N	R	U	N
S	N	A	I	T	P	Y	G	E	E	A
S	M	H	A	V	P	E	D	L	A	R
E	C	A	N	N	I	P	O	L	E	A
J	O	N	A	T	H	A	N	E	T	T

25

1 Who went to a ball and had to be home by midnight?
2 Who was swallowed by a whale?
3 Which is the biggest of the Channel Islands?
4 What form of Government does the United Kingdom have?
5 What do soldiers live in?
6 Which is the largest river in the world?
7 Who were the people Jesus called 'whited sepulchres'?
8 What do twenty-four sheets of writing paper make?
9 Who wrote the poem *Don Juan*?
10 What is a private soldier in the Royal Engineers called?
11 Which American state is called the Blue Grass state?
12 What is one-hundredth of a rouble?
13 'We can scarcely hate anyone that we know,' wrote which nineteenth-century essayist?
14 Which board game ends with checkmate?
15 Whose downfall was foretold by the writing on the wall?
16 What is fortune-telling from hands called?
17 What is the grub of the cranefly called?
18 Which Indian group is descended from Persians who fled from religious persecution to India?
19 What is a highly salted and garlic-flavoured Italian sausage called?
20 In classical legend what was the name of a woman who prophesied under the inspiration of a deity?
21 What is the name for a South African antelope resembling the elk?
22 What is the name for a soldier who may go to sea?
23 Which large snake crushes its victims?
24 What is the fortieth wedding anniversary called?

A	S	E	E	S	I	R	A	H	P	R
G	E	R	B	I	L	M	M	A	A	E
U	I	A	P	B	E	I	A	Z	I	V
Y	R	U	B	Y	A	C	Z	L	P	L
Y	E	Q	P	L	T	A	O	I	A	I
K	P	S	A	S	H	H	N	T	L	S
C	P	A	R	S	E	E	O	T	M	K
U	A	L	L	E	R	E	D	N	I	C
T	S	E	I	H	J	N	O	T	S	A
N	B	H	A	C	A	I	O	E	T	R
E	N	N	M	L	C	R	M	R	R	R
K	O	P	E	C	K	A	G	I	Y	A
J	R	C	N	G	E	M	T	U	N	B
D	I	C	T	A	T	O	R	Q	S	Y

26

1 Which football team besides Liverpool is based in Liverpool?
2 Who provides our bread?
3 Which English county is furthest west?
4 What is the outback of Australia sometimes called?
5 What breed of dog can fetch a bird that's been shot?
6 What is another name for the antirrhinum?
7 What is the capital of Australia?
8 Which ocean stretches from Africa to Indonesia?
9 Which gold coin was once worth a pound?
10 Which bird is associated with Christmas?
11 Which German city is divided between East and West?
12 Hans Christian ——; can you complete the story-teller's name?
13 On which of the Great Lakes does Cleveland stand?
14 What is another name for the Devil?
15 Who was King Arthur's Queen?
16 What is a South American ranch called?
17 Which is the largest of the Greek islands?
18 Which King of Portugal was called The Navigator?
19 Of which county is Exeter the county town?
20 Who is the patron saint of fishermen?
21 What is the capital of Cuba?
22 In which decisive battle of the Civil War in 1645 were the Royalists routed?
23 Which line has no end?
24 When does a young man's fancy lightly turn to thoughts of love, according to the poet Tennyson?

B	A	K	E	R	C	D	E	V	O	N
C	A	R	L	E	O	N	H	N	G	O
S	N	L	A	T	N	A	I	I	N	I
N	E	C	I	R	C	L	E	N	I	L
A	S	R	L	I	R	R	R	D	D	L
P	R	A	E	E	E	E	M	I	L	A
D	E	N	B	V	T	V	B	A	O	D
R	D	A	O	E	E	E	W	N	G	E
A	N	S	P	R	I	N	G	A	A	M
G	A	E	O	T	R	R	I	N	Q	C
O	S	B	S	O	E	E	A	U	I	O
N	I	Y	C	N	W	V	E	H	G	K
N	O	I	T	C	A	E	R	E	N	E
Y	R	N	E	H	N	N	N	J	A	R

27

1 Who discovered the New World?
2 What sort of hat is worn by hussars?
3 What vehicle has to be lifted and pushed?
4 Which river forms part of the boundary between Devon and Cornwall?
5 What is an Irish girl called?
6 Who wrote *Peter Pan*?
7 Which plant is chiefly associated with ice cream flavouring?
8 What is a person called who enters a house to steal?
9 What is the name of the Queen's second son?
10 What sort of game bird sounds like a complaint?
11 What is the name of the peninsula between the Dee and the Mersey?
12 In what sort of house does a priest live?
13 What is the principal London airport called?
14 On which river does Leicester stand?
15 Which Elizabethan explorer and colonist was also an author and poet?
16 What is the capital of the Bahamas?
17 Which legendary figure sold his soul to the devil?
18 Which famous holiday island lies to the south of the Bay of Naples?
19 Which seaside town added Regis to its name after George V stayed there?
20 What did the ancient Egyptians write on?
21 Which creature in the fable beat the hare in a race?
22 Which river runs into the Bristol Channel?
23 What cereal is used for brewing and cattle feed?
24 Which cloth comes from the wool of an animal like the llama?

N	R	E	V	E	S	Y	L	H	E	D
C	O	L	L	E	E	N	I	G	E	R
O	N	N	N	L	T	T	A	I	R	A
W	G	I	R	O	C	N	H	E	E	C
I	O	A	T	S	O	A	A	L	A	I
R	B	R	O	S	L	S	P	A	L	R
R	P	G	R	O	U	S	E	R	L	E
A	A	A	T	A	M	A	R	G	I	L
L	P	A	O	R	B	U	F	R	N	A
P	Y	D	I	T	U	L	R	U	A	N
A	R	A	S	I	S	A	E	B	V	D
C	U	N	E	C	B	O	N	E	A	R
A	S	A	L	L	Y	K	C	A	H	E
N	I	C	H	E	A	T	H	R	O	W

28

1 Who was Prime Minister after Chamberlain?
2 Which country lies to the north of Namibia?
3 Which place in Greece is associated with a legendary oracle?
4 Which is the highest mountain in Wales?
5 Which name forms part of three counties?
6 What is another name for the halcyon?
7 Who sailed single-handed round the world in *Gipsy Moth IV*?
8 Which freshwater fish has black or red spots?
9 What is a senior Government minister called?
10 What code is used in telegraphy?
11 Where is the Queen's University?
12 What is made by grinding corn?
13 Which drink is made from beans?
14 Which instrument is an octave higher than an ordinary flute?
15 What is President Reagan's first name?
16 What is a bluish-white metal that resists corrosion?
17 Which architectural form is associated with Egypt?
18 In which part of France did the Allies land on D-day in 1944?
19 Which African lake is bordered by the state of Malawi?
20 Which name is associated with a collection of marbles?
21 Which city on the River Dee was once a Roman fortress?
22 Which state of the USA was settled by Mormons?
23 Where was a congress held in 1814 after Napoleon's exile to Elba?
24 What is a collection of stories about gods and heroes called?

D	L	A	N	O	R	M	A	N	D	Y
E	R	I	H	S	K	R	O	Y	R	R
Z	C	E	C	A	N	L	G	A	A	E
I	I	T	H	O	O	O	T	S	H	L
H	R	N	I	C	L	E	W	A	C	L
P	Y	E	C	O	R	R	T	D	R	A
L	L	I	H	C	R	U	H	C	O	G
E	P	T	E	S	O	O	L	V	S	N
D	Y	S	S	R	I	L	E	I	S	I
M	R	I	T	S	A	F	L	E	B	T
O	A	T	E	A	L	O	G	N	A	T
R	M	N	R	I	D	R	I	N	T	I
S	I	E	N	G	E	U	N	A	I	N
E	D	D	E	A	R	M	I	L	K	K

29

1 Who was first president of the USA?
2 What is the capital of Poland?
3 What was a Stuart claimant to the throne of England called?
4 Which Crimean War commander had an overcoat named after him?
5 What is a member of the upper house of the US Congress called?
6 Who wrote the opera *The Barber of Seville*?
7 What is the Papal territory inside Rome called?
8 Who were associated with the Medes in unchangeable laws?
9 Who was the legendary Red Indian chief about whom Longfellow wrote a poem?
10 Which republic in the British Commonwealth is based on a great seaport?
11 Which metropolitan borough is joined to Newcastle by the Tyne bridges?
12 What is the musical word for a lively, busy movement?
13 Which Greek goddess handed out divine retribution?
14 Which wading bird has a long curved bill?
15 Name the hero in Scott's poem *Marmion* who carried off a girl just before her wedding.
16 Mark —— created the characters Tom Sawyer and Huckleberry Finn; what is his name?
17 Which town and monastery in Italy was the scene of a great battle in 1944?
18 Blimp and Bogy share which Army rank?
19 How many oaks suggest a town in Kent?
20 In which month does the late summer bank holiday fall in Britain and Northern Ireland?
21 What is the land on the west side of the Atlantic?
22 Who commands a ship?
23 What colour ranges from pink to deep crimson?
24 What thread comes from a plant?

S	C	S	H	E	L	L	A	C	E	L
D	A	E	H	S	E	T	A	G	D	E
R	P	V	L	W	A	R	S	A	W	N
Y	T	E	N	I	N	C	I	A	I	O
E	A	N	R	A	A	A	S	E	N	L
R	I	I	T	S	C	H	E	R	Z	O
E	N	I	S	I	I	T	M	R	E	C
G	O	I	U	N	T	A	E	O	R	H
N	N	O	G	G	A	W	N	S	O	I
O	E	T	U	A	V	A	A	S	T	N
C	O	W	A	P	O	I	L	I	A	V
N	O	T	T	O	C	H	G	N	N	A
E	A	C	I	R	E	M	A	I	E	R
R	E	D	N	E	T	E	R	P	S	I

30

1 In schools and universities what is the term before Christmas called?
2 After Calcutta and Bombay, which is the biggest port in India?
3 What is a small, dark purple plum called?
4 What is sometimes called the granite city?
5 What is a collector of coins called?
6 Haddon Hall and Chatsworth are near which Derbyshire town?
7 Which is the last book of the Old Testament?
8 What is a long clay pipe called?
9 Which Nottingham official was Robin Hood's enemy?
10 Porthos and Aramis were two of the Three Musketeers; who was the third?
11 Which is the lightest of all known substances?
12 What is associated with faith and charity?
13 What is obtained by burning wood?
14 Which drink is made from honey?
15 Which is the chief port of Israel?
16 Who was Prime Minister before Callaghan?
17 What are the treeless plains of South America called?
18 Which was the kingdom of the underworld in Greek mythology?
19 What is a member of a wandering community called?
20 Which hills lie in Avon and Somerset?
21 What is a person who works in stone called?
22 What is another name for the cougar?
23 Which tree is cultivated for its oily fruit?
24 Gilbert —— was a famous naturalist; can you complete the name?

S	A	P	M	A	P	L	I	N	L	L
A	A	E	U	I	I	C	O	R	A	L
R	A	M	D	S	L	H	K	O	E	E
D	V	N	L	L	C	U	C	D	P	W
A	E	U	W	E	H	R	A	O	N	E
M	N	M	A	L	A	C	H	I	I	K
S	E	I	Y	H	R	H	A	I	F	A
O	G	S	C	A	D	W	C	F	P	B
N	O	M	A	D	I	A	I	I	U	E
O	R	A	A	E	E	R	T	E	M	R
S	D	T	T	S	E	D	I	V	A	D
L	Y	I	O	H	O	E	Z	I	P	E
I	H	S	S	O	O	N	E	L	O	E
W	E	T	H	E	R	S	N	O	W	N

31

1 Which great Dutch painter was born in Leyden and lived in Amsterdam?
2 Prince Richard is a royal Duke – of where?
3 This Beauty is a butterfly; name the place.
4 What was the name for any large sailing ship?
5 Which rank in the army is indicated by three stripes?
6 Where was an Archduke assassinated in 1914, starting the First World War?
7 Which instrument measures atmospheric pressure?
8 Which football club suggests a lot of guns?
9 Which instrument has five strings and a body covered with parchment?
10 Who stabs herself to death after her lover has poisoned himself in a play by Shakespeare?
11 Which castle is a royal residence?
12 Which very important railway junction is in Cheshire?
13 Name an African people found in Natal.
14 What is a thicket of dwarf trees in the west of America called?
15 Of what nationality are the citizens of Teheran?
16 Of which country was Hamlet prince?
17 What sort of animals traditionally draw Santa Claus' sleigh?
18 Which animal has the hump?
19 In which building would you find an ambassador?
20 What is a large black or green African snake called?
21 Who is a tragic king in a play by Shakespeare?
22 Which seat is the old Turkish name for a council of state?
23 Where do cowboys put on a show of skill?
24 Which opera by Verdi concerns an Egyptian princess?

L	A	R	R	A	P	A	H	C	E	R
E	U	I	O	K	E	I	R	L	C	O
M	W	F	S	E	R	G	E	A	N	T
A	A	I	D	A	M	A	M	B	A	C
C	T	D	N	A	R	B	M	E	R	E
N	R	I	I	S	E	A	A	N	F	R
O	A	E	W	R	T	R	J	S	E	I
N	Z	V	W	E	S	O	D	E	S	D
N	U	E	I	E	E	M	N	T	V	Y
E	L	L	N	D	C	E	I	O	N	O
L	U	A	O	N	U	T	W	N	A	J
J	L	R	U	I	O	E	A	A	L	N
L	I	O	N	E	L	R	D	I	C	A
P	A	M	I	R	G	L	I	P	U	B

32

1 Which island forms the Malagasy Republic?
2 Who composed the music for the ballets *Swan Lake* and *The Sleeping Beauty*?
3 Which mountain chain lies along the west coast of South America?
4 What is the Scottish word for a southerner?
5 In which American state is the city of Little Rock?
6 King Charles is a variety of which breed of dog?
7 In which of Shakespeare's plays does Caliban appear?
8 Which country lies between Algeria and Libya?
9 What was the name of a great merchant ship from Ragusa or Venice?
10 Britain's first Labour Prime Minister was —— MacDonald. What was his other name?
11 What is the present-day value of a florin?
12 Which town in Kent lies across the River Thames from Tilbury?
13 Which Trojan warrior was the son of King Priam and Hecuba?
14 Where was the gaol about which Oscar Wilde wrote a ballad?
15 What sort of leather has a napped surface?
16 What sort of numerals are formed by letters?
17 What sort of beard is a small tuft on the chin?
18 —— *Doone* is the name of a famous book by R. D. Blackmore; can you complete the title?
19 Which musical instrument has a collection of pipes?
20 Can you complete the name of the well-known film star —— Peck?
21 What structure carries a road or railway over a valley?
22 Which is the longest river in Africa after the Nile?
23 Who was the hero of Virgil's great poem?
24 Can you complete the name of the Glasgow football club —— Thistle?

R	A	M	S	A	Y	L	L	E	K	T
U	O	P	T	E	N	P	E	N	C	E
O	H	M	S	L	E	I	G	H	I	M
H	E	A	A	E	E	L	A	N	T	P
G	C	D	T	N	O	I	N	U	R	E
R	T	A	A	R	K	A	N	S	A	S
E	O	G	N	O	C	I	G	A	P	T
G	R	A	V	E	S	E	N	D	P	Y
O	O	S	I	I	S	E	I	D	C	S
R	K	C	A	R	D	S	D	N	I	O
Y	M	A	D	E	I	R	A	N	R	G
T	A	R	U	L	N	C	E	S	A	R
A	I	S	C	A	A	E	R	V	L	A
S	S	E	T	V	Y	R	A	N	A	C

33

1 With which invention is the name of Baird associated?
2 Who is my lady in a song said to have been written by Henry VIII?
3 Which animal is sometimes known as the hunting leopard?
4 Which British Captain landed at Botany Bay?
5 In the books by P. G. Wodehouse what is the name of Bertie Wooster's manservant?
6 Who swam the Hellespont to visit Hero?
7 What is associated with the hammer in the Russian flag?
8 Which North Yorkshire town is a famous inland health resort?
9 Which country lies to the south of Egypt?
10 What did the daring young man fly through the air on?
11 Where did the Barber live in Rossini's opera?
12 'That's the wise ——; he sings each song twice over,' wrote the poet Browning of which bird?
13 What is the Italian word meaning Mister?
14 Which woolly garment is named after the man who led the charge of the Light Brigade?
15 Can you find the name of an opera by Verdi?
16 On which river does the city of Avignon stand?
17 Who wrote the famous poem to Autumn?
18 Which anthropoid ape is found in Borneo?
19 What is the name for a nearly cylindrical military hat with peak and plume?
20 Which town is mentioned in the famous Welsh marching song 'Men of ——'?
21 Which volcanic island was the scene of a huge eruption in 1883?
22 Which sign of the Zodiac is a bull?
23 What is the name of the American award given to films and film stars?
24 The Beatles' drummer's first name?

A	H	C	T	O	C	S	P	T	O	E
L	S	T	H	A	T	E	H	R	H	T
T	A	U	R	U	S	I	S	A	L	A
O	B	S	U	O	E	E	T	P	K	G
N	O	I	S	I	V	E	L	E	T	O
N	T	C	H	I	E	A	P	Z	P	R
I	A	K	L	H	E	O	T	E	C	R
R	G	L	C	C	L	T	R	O	A	A
J	E	E	V	E	S	A	O	C	R	H
S	O	A	V	L	N	K	N	E	D	E
T	U	N	G	R	E	A	G	A	I	N
A	E	D	A	A	E	R	I	N	G	O
E	V	E	A	H	R	K	S	I	A	H
K	O	R	A	N	G	U	T	A	N	R

34

1 Admiral of the Fleet killed by a bomb in Ireland in August 1979 — who was he?
2 Hero of many books about the Navy in Nelson's time written by C. S. Forester – who is he?
3 Which Duke led a rebellion against James II in 1685?
4 In which region of Scotland is Edinburgh?
5 Who is the Emperor of Japan in a Gilbert and Sullivan opera?
6 What are the drifting organisms in seas, lakes and rivers called?
7 What is a small metal flute called?
8 Which Roman emperor gave his name to a wall across the north of England?
9 John —— was the author of *The Pilgrim's Progress*; what was his name?
10 What is the lowest rank in the infantry?
11 On which river does Baghdad stand?
12 In which American state is the city of Omaha?
13 In the nursery rhyme which creatures were baked in a pie?
14 What is a sailing boat with a single mast and fixed bowsprit called?
15 What green plant would you find in a salad?
16 What colour is brownish crimson?
17 Which famous public school did Churchill attend?
18 What is a creature called that lives on another?
19 What sort of person was Barnacle Bill?
20 Who was Joseph's younger son and founder of a tribe?
21 What thin glossy silk stuff is sometimes used to make party dresses?
22 Which colourless inert gas was discovered in the atmosphere in 1894?
23 What is a stray calf without a brand called?
24 Which precious stone is generally red?

H	O	P	N	M	I	A	R	H	P	E
A	M	R	A	T	E	F	F	A	T	Y
N	A	I	H	T	O	L	R	R	L	T
N	V	V	K	T	I	A	M	R	F	R
A	E	A	A	A	S	G	A	O	E	A
S	R	T	R	I	D	E	R	W	T	E
O	I	E	T	G	R	O	O	I	I	H
H	C	E	S	A	I	L	O	R	S	T
A	K	S	A	R	B	E	N	L	H	U
D	P	L	A	N	K	T	O	N	B	O
R	A	O	R	E	C	T	N	I	A	M
I	S	O	G	T	A	U	R	U	R	N
A	H	P	O	T	L	C	E	R	O	O
N	A	Y	N	U	B	E	V	B	N	M

35

1 Which murdered dictator is the subject of a Shakespeare play?
2 Which great ship hit an iceberg and sank in 1912?
3 What is another name for the Holy Land?
4 Where does the Tweed join the Teviot?
5 Which planet is nearest the sun?
6 Which machine clears and levels land?
7 What is a native of Brittany called?
8 Who wrote *Auld Lang Syne*?
9 Which island was discovered by Columbus and captured by Britain from Spain?
10 There's a university college of which name in Oxford, Cambridge and Dublin?
11 What sort of horse would you associate with the ragtag?
12 Which important Iranian oil centre was heavily damaged in the war between Iraq and Iran?
13 Which former Australian mandated territory is now joined with Papua?
14 What name was given to Simon Bolivar, hero of South American independence struggles?
15 Which province of Italy is noted for its cheese?
16 Which orange-pink substance is formed from the skeletons of tiny sea-creatures?
17 Where did the poet Browning wish to be in April?
18 Which type of brick is named after a village in Cambridgeshire?
19 What sort of headgear is worn by paratroops?
20 Victoria is a variety of what sort of fruit?
21 Which country in South America was formerly Dutch Guiana?
22 Who wrote a book about an imaginary country called *Erewhon*? Samuel ——.
23 What substance is made from tanned hide?
24 In Shakespeare's *The Tempest* who is Prospero's slave?

D	S	U	R	I	N	A	M	R	A	P
N	U	O	E	N	R	O	B	A	A	L
A	M	S	H	Y	L	R	T	L	T	U
L	M	R	T	T	I	A	E	E	O	M
G	E	O	A	I	A	S	R	G	R	B
N	R	T	E	N	T	E	D	O	U	B
E	C	A	L	I	B	A	N	R	C	U
W	U	R	N	R	O	C	N	U	R	L
G	R	E	A	T	B	S	O	I	A	L
U	Y	B	D	Z	B	U	T	O	C	D
I	T	I	A	H	Y	I	T	S	K	O
N	N	L	B	V	O	L	E	L	N	Z
E	R	C	A	P	A	U	L	E	E	E
A	C	I	A	M	A	J	F	K	L	R

36

1. Which British Commonwealth country is a Commonwealth in itself?
2. Which is England's largest lake?
3. What form of transport is held up by downward jets?
4. Where is Leeds cricket ground?
5. Which river in Virginia, USA, is the subject of a sea shanty?
6. Can you find the name of a smoked German sausage?
7. Which metal is used in nuclear power stations?
8. Which constellation is named after Cassiopeia's daughter, who was chained to a rock?
9. Who rescued and married Cassiopeia's daughter?
10. Which Biblical city was destroyed by Joshua?
11. Which town in the Isle of Wight is famous for yachting?
12. What is an establishment of monks called?
13. What is the name of the great French fortress on the Meuse?
14. What was the old name for a British soldier?
15. Who was the subject of a biography by Boswell?
16. Which Italian city was famous for its violin makers?
17. Which form of Hindustani is the official literary language of Pakistan?
18. Which breed of dog can show where the game is?
19. Which flower is associated with shrinking?
20. Which seaside resort is officially called Great?
21. Which musical instrument suggests ice-cream?
22. Which country stretches to the southernmost part of South America?
23. Which bird did Noah send out from the ark?
24. Which animal is associated with spying?

T	F	A	R	C	R	E	V	O	H	C
P	R	N	P	M	M	V	I	A	A	R
E	A	A	Y	O	U	O	O	B	E	E
R	U	I	E	R	I	D	L	R	A	M
S	N	R	L	T	N	N	E	E	I	O
E	N	O	G	A	A	M	T	V	R	N
U	R	A	N	D	R	O	M	E	D	A
S	O	E	I	E	U	T	C	R	R	S
C	H	A	D	L	R	E	S	D	I	T
S	C	N	A	L	D	N	N	U	E	E
E	I	B	E	A	U	R	A	N	A	R
W	R	I	H	T	U	O	M	R	A	Y
O	E	A	B	I	R	C	H	I	L	E
C	J	O	H	N	S	O	N	S	I	B

1 Which small rodent is valued for its soft grey fur?
2 Which teacake is named after a girl who once sold them?
3 In which American state is the city of Portland?
4 Which plant resembling an onion is used to flavour dishes?
5 Who succeeded Wilson as Prime Minister?
6 What is the Kohinoor?
7 Which large sword was formerly used by Scottish highlanders?
8 On which river do Vienna, Budapest and Belgrade stand?
9 Which town is joined to Rochester and Gillingham?
10 What small black and white bird makes a sound like clattering pebbles?
11 What is the Norwegian Parliament called?
12 Which mountains are found in the north of Italy?
13 What is the English form of the Irish name Caitlin?
14 Which bird lays eggs in other birds' nests?
15 What was the name for a Scandinavian pirate of the eighth to tenth centuries?
16 What feast commemorates the Israelites being spared by the angel of death?
17 What is a Scottish landowner called?
18 What sort of chair was picked up and carried by two men?
19 Who is in charge of the nurses in a hospital?
20 What is a mass of ice creeping down a mountainside called?
21 Which buccaneer was knighted by Charles II for his exploits against the Spaniards?
22 What is another name for the Norway lobster?
23 What is the name for a maze or a building with many twisting passages?
24 Which Roman poet was famous for his odes?

T	N	A	S	A	E	P	R	I	S	M
E	O	R	E	G	O	N	A	N	E	A
P	R	G	T	L	C	O	N	A	D	H
A	T	O	I	A	A	U	K	N	A	T
R	A	M	M	B	L	I	O	C	N	A
A	M	L	O	Y	L	M	B	E	U	H
P	C	I	L	R	A	G	E	S	B	C
A	R	L	O	I	G	L	R	T	E	E
S	A	Y	D	N	H	A	C	O	C	N
S	W	E	L	T	A	C	N	R	A	O
O	F	N	A	H	N	I	N	T	R	T
V	I	K	I	N	G	E	I	I	O	S
E	S	R	R	A	E	R	D	N	H	A
R	H	O	D	Y	R	L	O	G	I	C

38

1 Which island forms the commercial centre of New York?
2 Who was Supreme Allied Commander in Europe during the last war?
3 Which Shakespeare play is about jealousy?
4 What was an adventurer who plundered the Spanish in the West Indies called?
5 Whom did General Wolfe defeat at Quebec?
6 What is associated with faith and hope?
7 Which place in Cornwall is thought to be where King Arthur had his seat?
8 What unit of currency is used in the USA?
9 Which girl is associated with Peter Pan?
10 What underwater weapon is used to sink an enemy ship?
11 *The Flute Player* is a famous picture by which great nineteenth-century French painter?
12 What is a non-Catholic Christian called?
13 Which Mediterranean evergreen shrub has red, white or pink flowers?
14 What are the feelers of some insects and crustaceans called?
15 What relation was Cain to Abel?
16 Sir Thomas —— wrote the book *Utopia* and was beheaded in the reign of Henry VIII. Who?
17 Which town is famous for horse-racing?
18 What is the name of a famous bridge in Venice?
19 What is the big cash prize?
20 Who cut off Samson's hair?
21 Which animal was once thought to hunt a lion's prey for him?
22 Thomas was a great headmaster of Rugby school; Matthew, his son, was a famous poet. What was the family name?
23 Name an African or Indian hand-beaten drum.
24 What class of Royal Navy ship was used to defeat the German battleship *Graf Spee*?

T	O	P	K	C	A	J	M	A	C	Y
O	Y	T	I	R	A	H	C	O	O	D
M	B	U	C	C	A	N	E	E	R	N
T	U	R	K	A	M	P	A	E	R	E
O	L	A	O	N	A	R	W	M	A	W
M	L	A	C	T	N	O	M	D	L	M
O	O	L	L	E	H	T	O	R	L	A
R	R	E	D	N	A	E	L	O	O	R
R	E	S	E	N	T	S	R	F	D	K
O	I	S	L	A	T	T	T	L	E	E
W	I	A	I	E	A	A	O	E	P	T
E	A	R	L	U	N	N	R	M	R	I
L	A	T	A	T	R	T	O	A	O	N
L	O	C	H	A	O	C	C	C	T	G

39

1 Whose name is associated with elegant eighteenth-century furniture?
2 Which is the longest main line railway tunnel in the world?
3 Which animal in Old Testament times symbolically carried the sins of the people?
4 What was the earlier name for a Liberal?
5 Where are the British lawn tennis championships held . . .?
6 . . . and who won the singles championship there four times in succession?
7 What is the name of the old fortress and palace of Granada?
8 Who was the Roman goddess of love?
9 Which great English novelist was born in Poland?
10 Which Canadian territory had a gold rush?
11 Which famous old cricketer was a doctor?
12 —— Court was the palace Wolsey gave to Henry VIII. Can you complete the name?
13 Which book of the Old Testament comes after Zephaniah?
14 What cushioned seat describes the old Turkish empire?
15 What is the capital of Spain?
16 Which French painter is famous for pictures of ballet girls?
17 Which wine-growing province of France was once an independent monarchy?
18 Which is the principal port of Chile?
19 What is a carriage with a folding top called?
20 Which country did the Romans call Hibernia?
21 What relation was William III to Mary II?
22 What skirt does a ballet dancer wear?
23 Which is the RAF airfield nearest the centre of London?
24 Which word meaning hard work is the word for a coach in France?

A	R	B	M	A	H	L	A	T	A	M
D	A	K	O	T	A	O	A	L	L	A
A	T	T	C	R	G	O	G	O	L	D
V	L	W	H	I	G	H	E	H	I	R
E	A	U	I	E	A	C	U	T	N	I
N	O	L	P	M	I	S	T	R	A	D
U	R	A	P	N	B	S	U	O	M	I
S	C	T	E	A	U	L	T	N	O	L
S	O	R	N	I	R	L	E	A	T	I
N	E	D	D	E	G	A	S	D	T	G
B	S	A	A	C	U	N	I	O	O	E
I	R	E	L	A	N	D	Y	S	O	N
T	U	N	E	R	D	A	R	N	O	C
E	N	E	R	G	Y	U	K	O	N	E

40

1 Who was defeated at Waterloo?
2 Who was Britain's greatest admiral?
3 What is the capital of Nova Scotia?
4 Which swan makes a throaty sound?
5 Who is a villain in one of the James Bond books?
6 What sort of goat has long silky wool?
7 What is the name of the Duke of Edinburgh?
8 Which place in Greater London is the name of a breed of poultry?
9 In *A Midsummer Night's Dream* who is Queen of the fairies?
10 Of which country is Helsinki the capital?
11 Which sea bird has a brightly coloured beak like a parrot's?
12 What are Great Britain and Russia parts of?
13 In eastern countries what is the seclusion of women called?
14 What breed of horse has a gold-coloured coat and a white mane and tail?
15 Which king is remembered for being very wise?
16 Which animal is used to get rabbits out of burrows?
17 Which American state is nearest to the USSR?
18 What does a Jew call someone who is not a Jew?
19 What sort of dog is an outcast?
20 What sort of aircraft was a Spitfire?
21 With what sort of tree is the Lebanon associated?
22 Which land of ancient Greece is associated with a carefree, happy life?
23 What is the organisation to which British trade unions are affiliated?
24 What Services entertainment is held annually in Edinburgh?

P	U	R	D	A	H	H	A	R	P	O
A	R	R	A	B	A	T	L	L	A	O
R	W	E	N	D	A	L	A	S	L	T
C	O	N	G	R	E	S	S	E	O	T
A	M	O	O	N	M	C	K	X	M	A
D	N	R	R	A	I	N	A	T	I	T
I	U	E	A	P	U	F	F	I	N	G
A	D	P	I	O	I	I	D	E	O	R
P	N	O	S	L	E	N	O	L	M	I
I	O	O	A	E	U	L	G	I	O	N
L	M	H	N	O	R	A	F	T	L	G
I	L	W	P	N	O	N	I	N	O	O
H	A	I	R	A	P	D	S	E	S	N
P	F	E	R	R	E	T	H	G	I	F

Answers

Words

1 1 Victoria 2 Fingal 3 Walter 4 Civet 5 Amsterdam 6 Machiavelli 7 Cavaliers 8 Cairo 9 Israel 10 Purcell 11 Cancer 12 Halifax 13 Choctaw 14 Down 15 Faraday 16 Largo 17 Cato 18 Runcorn 19 Chain 20 Diameter 21 Slate 22 Webb 23 Reactor 24 Coventry

2 1 Gainsborough 2 Zimbabwe 3 Atlantic 4 Alsatian 5 Minster 6 Balsam 7 Caballero 8 Manitoba 9 Saladin 10 Belgium 11 Wilhelmina 12 Hamburg 13 Koran 14 Juliet 15 Alaska 16 Topaz 17 Eastbourne 18 Orion 19 Sacramento 20 Gules 21 Eton 22 Krone 23 Bristol 24 Jute

3 1 Hannibal 2 Whittington 3 Levant 4 Bamboo 5 Romanies 6 Nottingham 7 Dreadnought 8 Gambia 9 Martingale 10 Goliath 11 Trent 12 Greene 13 Montana 14 Cossack 15 Bottom 16 Tonga 17 Yak 18 Indigo 19 Tomato 20 Clevedon 21 Nougat 22 Gannet 23 Banana 24 Carnegie

4 1 Thatcher 2 Concertina 3 *King Lear* 4 *Imagination* 5 President 6 Bittern 7 Catherine 8 Triton 9 Peebles 10 Columbine 11 Ravenna 12 Anne 13 Captain 14 Canada 15 Demeter 16 Cuba 17 Manet 18 Dunedin 19 Trajan 20 Bassoon 21 Oporto 22 Iona 23 Anaconda 24 Preston

5 1 Beethoven 2 Leeds 3 *Carmen* 4 Benjamin 5 Peony 6 Jenner 7 Como 8 Ambassador 9 Mithras 10 China 11 Mouth-organ 12 Turner 13 Maine 14 Monmouth 15 Emma 16 Simenon 17 Dives 18 Diamond 19 Navarre 20 Calgary 21 Scott 22 Aaron 23 Balfour 24 Beverley

6 1 Churchill 2 Brazil 3 Bach 4 Tarzan 5 Cape Town 6 Date 7 Connemara 8 Taxidermist 9 Tanzania 10 Ziggurat 11 Algebra 12 Damascus 13 Marconi 14 Baltic 15 Reading 16 Astrakhan 17 Dingo 18 Burns 19 Iodine 20 Irene 21 Atlas 22 Wallace 23 Bermuda 24 Ouse

7 1 Andersen 2 Senegal 3 Soprano 4 Boycott 5 Newcastle 6 Calypso 7 Carthage 8 Belgrade 9 Sirius 10 Aesop 11 Monopoly 12 Mayor 13 Howdah 14 Cambridge 15 Detroit 16 Paul 17 Bloodhound 18 Hardy 19 German 20 Borrow 21 Wotan 22 Caroline 23 Rajah 24 Test-tube

8 1 Siberia 2 Chemistry 3 Rabelais 4 Dail 5 Samarkand 6 Corsair 7 April 8 Alabama 9 Barnacle 10 Cyprus 11 Coward 12 Doncaster 13 Bessemer 14 Bishop 15 Cobalt 16 Camembert 17 Iberia 18 Ariadne 19 Cotoneaster 20 Marryat 21 Ashanti 22 Gray 23 Italian 24 Nereid

9 1 Wellington 2 Bulgaria 3 Brigantine 4 Bonn 5 Tigris 6 Birmingham 7 Bunsen 8 Serbia 9 Apollo 10 Wagtail 11 Nippon 12 Winston 13 Parma 14 Breve 15 Tennessee 16 Bourbon 17 Shaw 18 Loire 19 Wesley 20 Basra 21 Hitler 22 Adelaide 23 Violin 24 Palermo

10 1 Armadillo 2 Conqueror 3 Damocles 4 Seattle 5 Samson 6 Ontario 7 Tristan 8 Hurlingham 9 Quicksilver 10 Lark 11 Verne 12 Siam 13 Carroll 14 Heron 15 Shakespeare 16 Amman 17 Black 18 Silver 19 Chesterfield 20 Carillon 21 Alligator 22 Jackson 23 Paris 24 Elvis

11 1 Cleopatra 2 Ostrich 3 Panama 4 Clive 5 Chancellor 6 Scarab 7 Stephen 8 Goodwin 9 Wilson 10 Guitar 11 Champagne 12 Hanoi 13 Asparagus 14 Armada 15 Plainsong 16 Ripon 17 Valentine 18 Chaplin 19 August 20 Thames 21 Chamberlain 22 Boston 23 Cain 24 France

12 1 Handel 2 Scarborough 3 Hengist 4 Woolsack 5 Boswell 6 Stoat 7 Centurion 8 Sceptre 9 Azores 10 Epistle 11 Hereward 12 Delta 13 Tudor 14 Pilchard 15 Dissenter 16 Otter 17 Buchan 18 Almond 19 Bede 20 Cambric 21 Cockatoo 22 Osier 23 Liszt 24 Sabre

13 1 Garibaldi 2 Madeira 3 Ferdinand 4 Casablanca 5 *Barnaby* 6 Einstein 7 Duckling 8 Sherbet 9 Houdini 10 Lira 11 Ethelred 12 Mark 13 Syria 14 Handlebar 15 *Dutchman* 16 Humber 17 Druids 18 Kettering 19 Marne 20 Babylon 21 Hood 22 Flute 23 Marie 24 Abacus

14 1 Comprehensive 2 Bath 3 Pennyweight 4 Athens 5 Leopard 6 Brighton 7 Lucknow 8 Kennet 9 Operator

10 Bartholomew 11 Brenner 12 Tirana 13 Roedean 14 Scampi 15 Margate 16 Satrap 17 Dentist 18 Piranha 19 Prescription 20 Rabat 21 Nash 22 Colon 23 Kerala 24 Lagoon

15 1 Vienna 2 Penguin 3 Antelope 4 Caractacus 5 Shantung 6 Horatio 7 Congress 8 Uranus 9 Accra 10 Caruso 11 Matterhorn 12 Carnation 13 Harpoon 14 Steppes 15 Gothic 16 Raccoon 17 Oslo 18 Countess 19 Provence 20 Ounce 21 Calvin 22 Taunton 23 Panorama 24 Seraph

16 1 Westminster 2 Snowdrop 3 Tyrol 4 Patrick 5 Greenland 6 Schumann 7 Worthing 8 Trowel 9 Peacock 10 Horseshoe 11 Eclipse 12 Oregon 13 *Rocket* 14 Eider 15 Parnassus 16 Gertrude 17 Rhine 18 Antlers 19 Saturn 20 Regiment 21 Cork 22 Wordsworth 23 Pennine 24 Buck

17 1 Mediterranean 2 Sherpa 3 Watt 4 Downing 5 Housman 6 Masefield 7 Molasses 8 Mohammed 9 Telescope 10 Robespierre 11 Hereford 12 Dove 13 Ottawa 14 Serpentine 15 Esau 16 Mistral 17 Serenade 18 Sheep 19 Microbe 20 Minehead 21 Pimento 22 Tosca 23 Ashdown 24 Gobi

18 1 Nightingale 2 Southampton 3 Stephenson 4 Guardian 5 Hamlet 6 Lion 7 Kettledrum 8 Pemmican 9 Mountaineer 10 Polka 11 Spinnaker 12 Satan 13 Beech 14 Kayak 15 Piccalilli 16 Katmandu 17 Bounty 18 Dodo 19 Oriel 20 Stavanger 21 Leda 22 Capstan 23 Plate 24 Dakota

19 1 Montgomery 2 Huron 3 Canary 4 Muscatel 5 Bronte 6 Cantata 7 Sarong 8 Mormons 9 Cricket 10 Frigate 11 Georgia 12 Monsoon 13 Cameroon 14 Carapace 15 Sycamore 16 Manchester 17 Mirage 18 Cinema 19 Ventnor 20 Orange 21 Furnace 22 Norman 23 Marrow 24 Circus

20 1 Boadicea 2 Coven 3 Canterbury 4 Sputnik 5 Biretta 6 Copenhagen 7 Elgar 8 Natal 9 Perry 10 Goya 11 Himalayas 12 Munich 13 Pippin 14 Pandora 15 Pinto 16 Ketch 17 Martin 18 Calico 19 Pitt 20 Apricot 21 Parrot 22 Tyrone 23 Davy 24 Cockatrice

21 1 Dickens 2 Stork 3 Moscow 4 Brahms 5 Blacksmith 6 Toronto 7 Wilde 8 Pensioners 9 Actress 10 *Musketeers* 11 Rook 12 Psalms 13 Skylark 14 Minnesota 15 Cypress 16 Pink 17 Nadir 18 Orpheus 19 Tokyo 20 West Ham 21 Corroboree 22 Kenya 23 Sparta 24 Arran

22 1 Huckleberry 2 Cabinet 3 Berengaria 4 Derby 5 Stockton 6 Darlington 7 Hobson 8 Venice 9 Perkins 10 Regent 11 Starboard 12 Antonio 13 Hastings 14 Chopper 15 Hero 16 Perch 17 Tobacco 18 Italy 19 Igloo 20 Mayfair 21 Bugle 22 Tyne 23 Antioch 24 Tangier

23 1 Hornbeam 2 Caledonia 3 Cromwell 4 Norway 5 Polygon 6 Charlotte 7 Torpedo 8 Viper 9 Sandal 10 Jasmine 11 Portugal 12 Empress 13 Genoa 14 Walnut 15 Clarinet 16 Koala 17 Cheviot 18 Coot 19 Goneril 20 Woodcock 21 Wear 22 Acacia 23 Ophir 24 Robert

24 1 Hippopotamus 2 Huntingdon 3 Tarantella 4 Oculist 5 Lilliput 6 Kowtow 7 Egyptians 8 Thanet 9 Cupid 10 Voltaire 11 Bloater 12 Olivia 13 Hemlock 14 Chimpanzee 15 Jonathan 16 Jessica 17 Patience 18 Whippet 19 Edam 20 Castile 21 Diana 22 Ezekiel 23 Rebecca 24 Pinnace

25 1 Cinderella 2 Jonah 3 Jersey 4 Parliament 5 Barracks 6 Amazon 7 Pharisees 8 Quire 9 Byron 10 Sapper 11 Kentucky 12 Kopeck 13 Hazlitt 14 Chess 15 Belshazzar 16 Palmistry 17 Leatherjacket 18 Parsee 19 Salami 20 Sibyl 21 Eland 22 Marine 23 Python 24 Ruby

26 1 Everton 2 Baker 3 Cornwall 4 Never-never land 5 Retriever 6 Snapdragon 7 Canberra 8 Indian 9 Sovereign 10 Robin 11 Berlin 12 Andersen 13 Erie 14 Belial 15 Guinevere 16 Hacienda 17 Crete 18 Henry 19 Devon 20 Peter 21 Havana 22 Naseby 23 Circle 24 Spring

27 1 Columbus 2 Busby 3 Wheelbarrow 4 Tamar 5 Colleen 6 Barrie 7 Vanilla 8 Burglar 9 Andrew 10 Grouse 11 Wirral 12 Parsonage 13 Heathrow 14 Soar 15 Raleigh 16 Nassau 17 Faust 18 Capri 19 Bognor 20 Papyrus 21 Tortoise 22 Severn 23 Barley 24 Alpaca

28 1 Churchill 2 Angola 3 Delphi 4 Snowdon 5 Yorkshire 6 Kingfisher 7 Chichester 8 Trout 9 Secretary 10 Morse 11 Belfast 12 Flour 13 Cocoa 14 Piccolo 15 Ronald 16 Zinc 17 Pyramid 18 Normandy 19 Nyasa 20 Elgin 21 Chester 22 Utah 23 Vienna 24 Mythology

29 1 Washington 2 Warsaw 3 Pretender 4 Raglan 5 Senator 6 Rossini 7 Vatican 8 Persians 9 Hiawatha 10 Singapore 11 Gateshead 12 Scherzo 13 Nemesis 14 Avocet 15 Lochinvar 16 Twain 17 Cassino 18 Colonel 19 Seven 20 August 21 America 22 Captain 23 Carnation 24 Cotton

30 1 Michaelmas 2 Madras 3 Damson 4 Aberdeen 5 Numismatist 6 Bakewell 7 Malachi 8 Churchwarden 9 Sheriff 10 Athos 11 Hydrogen 12 Hope 13 Charcoal 14 Mead 15 Haifa 16 Wilson 17 Pampas 18 Hades 19 Nomad 20 Mendip 21 Mason 22 Puma 23 Olive 24 White

31 1 Rembrandt 2 Gloucester 3 Camberwell 4 Windjammer 5 Sergeant 6 Sarajevo 7 Barometer 8 Arsenal 9 Banjo 10 Juliet 11 Windsor 12 Crewe 13 Zulu 14 Chaparral 15 Iranian 16 Denmark 17 Reindeer 18 Camel 19 Embassy 20 Mamba 21 Lear 22 Divan 23 Rodeo 24 *Aida*

32 1 Madagascar 2 Tchaikovsky 3 Andes 4 Sassenach 5 Arkansas 6 Spaniel 7 *Tempest* 8 Tunisia 9 Argosy 10 Ramsay 11 Tenpence 12 Gravesend 13 Hector 14 Reading 15 Suede 16 Roman 17 Goatee 18 *Lorna* 19 Organ 20 Gregory 21 Viaduct 22 Congo 23 Aeneas 24 Partick

33 1 Television 2 Greensleeves 3 Cheetah 4 Cook 5 Jeeves 6 Leander 7 Sickle 8 Harrogate 9 Sudan 10 Trapeze 11 Seville 12 Thrush 13 Signor 14 Cardigan 15 *Trovatore* 16 Rhone 17 Keats 18 Orang-utan 19 Shako 20 Harlech 21 Krakatoa 22 Taurus 23 Oscar 24 Ringo

34 1 Mountbatten 2 Hornblower 3 Monmouth 4 Lothian 5 Mikado 6 Plankton 7 Flageolet 8 Hadrian 9 Bunyan 10 Private 11 Tigris 12 Nebraska 13 Blackbirds

14 Sloop 15 Lettuce 16 Maroon 17 Harrow 18 Parasite 19 Sailor 20 Ephraim 21 Taffeta 22 Argon 23 Maverick 24 Garnet

35 1 Julius Caesar 2 Titanic 3 Palestine 4 Kelso 5 Mercury 6 Bulldozer 7 Breton 8 Burns 9 Jamaica 10 Trinity 11 Bobtail 12 Abadan 13 New Guinea 14 Liberator 15 Parma 16 Coral 17 England 18 Fletton 19 Beret 20 Plum 21 Surinam 22 Butler 23 Leather 24 Caliban

36 1 Australia 2 Windermere 3 Hovercraft 4 Headingley 5 Shenandoah 6 Mortadella 7 Uranium 8 Andromeda 9 Perseus 10 Jericho 11 Cowes 12 Monastery 13 Verdun 14 Redcoat 15 Johnson 16 Cremona 17 Urdu 18 Pointer 19 Violet 20 Yarmouth 21 Cornet 22 Chile 23 Dove 24 Mole

37 1 Chinchilla 2 Sally Lunn 3 Oregon 4 Garlic 5 Callaghan 6 Diamond 7 Claymore 8 Danube 9 Chatham 10 Stonechat 11 Storting 12 Dolomites 13 Kathleen 14 Cuckoo 15 Viking 16 Passover 17 Laird 18 Sedan 19 Matron 20 Glacier 21 Morgan 22 Crawfish 23 Labyrinth 24 Horace

38 1 Manhattan 2 Eisenhower 3 Othello 4 Buccaneer 5 Montcalm 6 Charity 7 Camelford 8 Dollar 9 Wendy 10 Torpedo 11 Corot 12 Protestant 13 Oleander 14 Antennae 15 Brother 16 More 17 Newmarket 18 Rialto 19 Jackpot 20 Delilah 21 Jackal 22 Arnold 23 Tom-tom 24 Cruiser

39 1 Chippendale 2 Simplon 3 Scapegoat 4 Whig 5 Wimbledon 6 Borg 7 Alhambra 8 Venus 9 Conrad 10 Yukon 11 Grace 12 Hampton 13 Haggai 14 Ottoman 15 Madrid 16 Degas 17 Burgundy 18 Valparaiso 19 Landau 20 Ireland 21 Husband 22 Tutu 23 Northolt 24 Diligence

40 1 Napoleon 2 Nelson 3 Halifax 4 Whooper 5 Goldfinger 6 Angora 7 Philip 8 Orpington 9 Titania 10 Finland 11 Puffin 12 Europe 13 Purdah 14 Palomino 15 Solomon 16 Ferret 17 Alaska 18 Gentile 19 Pariah 20 Fighter 21 Cedar 22 Arcadia 23 Congress 24 Tattoo

Diagrams

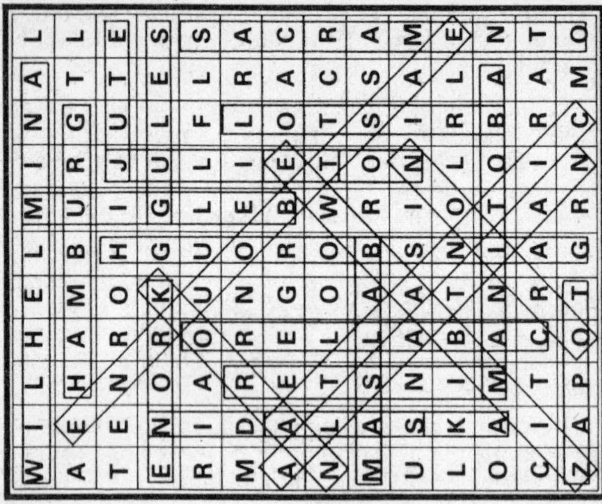

2

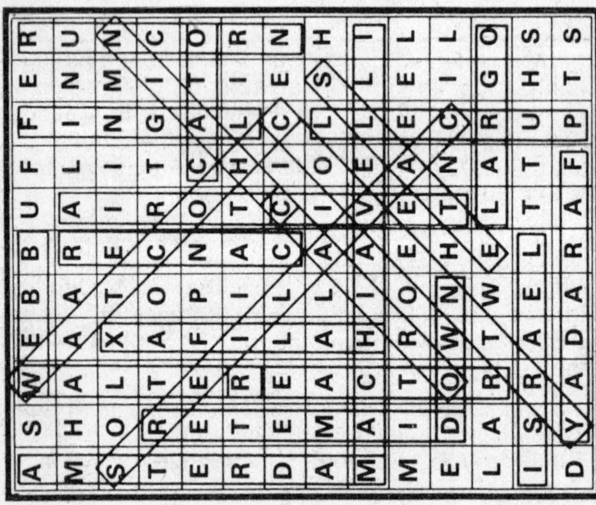

1

3

C	A	Y	A	K	C	A	S	S	O	C
A	A	N	T	N	A	V	E	L	T	M
G	L	B	C	I	R	I	L	T	A	A
N	L	A	B	I	N	N	A	H	M	R
O	O	M	B	A	E	T	G	G	O	T
T	A	B	M	N	G	N	R	U	T	I
G	O	O	U	A	I	E	T	O	T	N
N	R	O	N	T	E	R	S	N	O	G
I	P	N	T	N	C	T	U	D	B	A
T	E	O	E	O	E	H	E	A	A	L
T	N	U	O	M	A	V	E	E	N	E
I	N	G	L	L	E	M	A	R	A	C
H	T	A	I	L	O	G	I	D	N	I
W	A	T	C	H	A	I	R	M	A	N

4

C	T	E	N	A	N	N	E	V	A	R
O	A	L	C	O	H	O	L	N	I	E
L	R	T	T	A	R	I	I	O	R	T
U	Q	R	H	P	N	T	M	R	N	E
M	U	I	A	E	R	A	A	E	S	M
B	I	T	T	E	R	N	D	M	E	E
I	N	O	C	B	L	I	O	A	L	D
N	O	N	H	L	S	G	N	C	T	D
E	O	T	E	E	M	A	N	E	T	U
C	S	T	R	S	C	M	A	I	I	N
T	S	P	S	O	T	I	J	O	K	E
A	A	A	N	E	P	O	A	N	S	D
R	B	D	A	U	R	O	R	A	K	I
Y	A	B	U	C	A	P	T	A	I	N

5

S U N I M A J N E B E
R L C O O E N I A M Y
S E E O N E G L M E D
S S N N M E F A B D N
A S E R O O M E A I A
C R A R U L E I S A R
C C G R T T O C S M B
H A N I H C O C A O D
A M A O O T A R D N E
R P V M R L I O O D R
I E A E G N E M R I D
N O R A A I Y E R V N
E N R T N A N R D E U
T Y E L R E V E B S H

6

N W O T E P A C M C A
O A U S T R I A O I D
T L S E A O I N N T O
R L E T D N N O I L R
A A I I A E C N C A A
B C N Z M R A H A B B
B E N A A O U S N A I
I A R M S R N G I L Z
T A C M C R B I G L N
Y A O H U N T E T I A
B T I B S D I N G O Z
A L G N I D A E R L R
L A N A H K A R T S A
T S I M R E D I X A T

7

A	T	A	C	C	O	T	M	A	N	L
N	E	W	C	A	S	T	L	E	M	O
D	G	S	A	L	R	H	A	J	A	R
E	D	B	O	Y	C	O	T	T	Y	T
R	I	N	A	P	A	U	L	D	O	E
S	R	O	U	S	R	S	R	I	R	P
E	B	I	W	O	T	A	N	Y	N	T
N	M	N	S	P	H	N	N	L	T	E
E	A	U	U	H	A	D	W	O	H	S
G	C	M	I	Y	G	H	O	P	G	T
A	I	M	R	D	E	T	R	O	I	T
L	R	O	I	E	O	E	R	N	L	U
N	O	C	S	A	G	S	O	O	E	B
E	D	A	R	G	L	E	B	M	D	E

8

A	G	L	I	R	P	A	B	B	E	Y
S	U	E	E	K	O	R	E	H	C	R
I	I	T	N	A	H	S	A	P	E	T
A	L	H	R	T	S	R	N	T	I	S
L	D	E	M	E	I	S	S	E	N	I
E	I	A	M	A	B	A	L	A	C	M
B	E	E	D	A	E	M	N	R	C	E
A	R	N	C	N	R	A	E	S	O	H
R	E	E	O	A	I	R	C	M	B	C
N	N	T	W	L	A	K	Y	L	A	O
A	O	S	A	A	S	A	P	A	L	C
C	M	T	R	T	R	N	R	E	T	K
L	I	A	D	G	O	D	U	R	A	E
E	S	D	O	N	C	A	S	T	E	R

9

B	A	R	S	A	B	U	N	S	E	N
R	I	D	S	E	R	B	I	A	O	A
E	A	R	E	O	I	R	I	P	B	R
V	G	W	M	L	G	R	P	O	L	R
E	I	A	A	I	A	I	L	L	E	O
E	N	O	T	G	N	I	L	L	E	W
S	N	O	L	N	T	G	D	O	P	A
S	O	U	N	I	I	A	H	E	A	N
E	B	I	O	T	N	V	I	A	R	G
N	R	N	T	E	E	S	T	L	M	O
N	U	I	S	M	E	P	L	I	A	L
E	O	N	N	P	A	L	E	R	M	O
T	B	E	I	L	O	I	R	E	B	B
S	H	A	W	E	S	L	E	Y	A	R

10

E	C	P	S	E	L	C	O	M	A	D
S	H	A	K	E	S	P	E	A	R	E
N	N	R	R	R	O	N	N	H	A	D
A	O	I	A	R	A	O	R	G	I	L
M	L	S	P	O	O	L	E	N	L	E
M	A	H	M	T	E	L	V	I	S	I
A	A	R	M	A	D	I	L	L	O	F
N	R	I	T	G	S	R	I	R	O	R
O	K	M	S	I	E	A	S	U	I	E
S	I	P	B	L	A	C	K	H	R	T
K	T	L	G	L	T	N	C	E	A	S
C	E	G	N	A	T	S	I	R	T	E
A	U	E	K	A	L	B	U	O	N	H
J	U	R	O	R	E	U	O	N	O	C

11

N	O	L	Y	N	O	T	S	O	B	E
I	E	E	N	I	T	N	E	L	A	V
A	G	H	E	R	O	S	I	L	R	E
L	O	C	P	S	A	N	P	A	A	R
R	O	L	L	E	C	N	A	H	C	I
E	D	I	A	E	T	A	N	H	S	S
B	W	V	I	E	O	S	A	E	L	K
M	I	E	N	G	A	P	M	A	H	C
A	N	O	S	U	L	A	A	R	C	O
H	N	S	O	I	H	R	R	T	I	T
C	O	U	N	T	M	A	Q	U	R	N
O	P	G	G	A	U	G	U	S	T	A
M	I	R	D	R	S	U	I	S	S	U
F	R	A	N	C	E	S	S	U	O	Q

12

A	Z	O	R	E	S	O	P	M	O	C
T	H	I	S	T	R	T	U	D	O	R
L	C	E	P	I	S	T	L	E	T	E
E	L	C	R	I	E	E	P	E	A	T
D	N	E	G	E	L	R	I	E	K	N
N	R	N	W	R	W	C	T	D	C	E
A	E	T	O	S	E	A	H	I	O	S
H	G	U	O	R	O	B	R	A	C	S
C	A	R	L	T	O	B	E	D	R	I
U	L	I	S	N	M	A	N	E	T	D
B	I	O	A	A	D	N	O	M	L	A
A	S	N	C	N	B	E	D	E	L	L
N	Z	I	K	E	R	R	Y	T	A	S
A	T	C	Y	T	I	V	E	R	B	O

13

N	R	A	B	E	L	D	N	A	H	G
A	S	C	S	T	T	N	I	R	O	N
M	Q	N	Y	H	O	U	D	I	N	I
H	U	A	R	E	E	O	L	A	E	R
C	A	L	I	L	I	R	A	F	Y	E
T	R	B	A	R	N	A	B	Y	F	T
U	E	A	M	E	S	E	I	E	A	T
D	B	S	A	D	T	L	R	B	T	E
S	M	A	R	I	E	D	A	M	H	K
D	U	C	K	L	I	N	G	O	E	U
I	H	C	N	N	N	I	E	D	R	L
U	O	I	A	M	A	R	N	E	M	F
R	O	N	V	B	A	B	Y	L	O	N
D	D	T	E	E	A	S	T	O	N	E

14

T	H	G	I	E	W	Y	N	N	E	P
O	T	O	Y	K	E	R	A	L	A	R
L	A	P	R	W	V	I	S	O	R	E
I	B	E	O	M	I	R	H	O	L	S
P	A	R	T	A	S	A	E	S	Y	C
M	R	A	I	R	N	D	N	K	N	R
A	T	T	R	G	E	E	K	B	O	I
C	H	O	A	A	H	N	A	R	I	P
S	O	R	N	T	E	T	N	E	S	T
C	L	L	A	E	R	I	O	N	S	I
H	O	A	O	N	P	S	O	N	I	O
O	M	N	T	N	M	T	G	E	M	N
O	E	D	L	E	O	P	A	R	D	U
L	W	O	N	K	C	U	L	G	A	S

15

C	A	R	A	C	T	A	C	U	S	T
O	O	N	N	I	U	G	N	E	P	S
N	U	L	I	M	B	O	P	R	A	A
G	E	N	E	V	A	O	O	L	M	N
R	N	L	C	I	L	V	T	A	O	Y
E	A	U	Y	E	E	A	R	O	I	N
S	S	E	T	N	U	O	C	S	T	O
S	T	N	C	N	N	C	E	C	A	I
U	A	E	T	A	A	R	I	A	R	T
N	O	O	P	R	A	H	A	M	O	A
A	N	P	U	P	T	A	S	P	H	N
R	U	S	H	O	E	H	O	H	S	R
U	O	N	G	I	O	S	L	O	U	A
M	A	T	T	E	R	H	O	R	N	C

16

D	R	A	P	E	R	P	B	U	C	K
T	H	E	V	E	R	A	R	D	O	C
E	I	T	E	R	N	R	E	N	H	O
K	N	A	R	F	L	N	D	A	O	C
C	E	N	I	O	E	A	I	L	R	A
O	R	E	T	A	W	S	E	N	S	E
R	E	S	Y	A	O	S	R	E	E	P
K	G	E	R	T	R	U	D	E	S	O
C	I	C	O	E	T	S	S	R	H	R
I	M	A	L	A	H	P	U	G	O	D
R	E	T	S	N	I	M	T	S	E	W
T	N	S	I	L	N	O	G	E	R	O
A	T	U	C	I	G	A	R	T	I	N
P	R	E	N	N	A	M	U	H	C	S

17

E	L	B	M	U	M	H	M	S	O	T
R	N	L	I	I	I	P	E	E	H	S
R	A	I	S	I	N	R	D	P	A	E
E	S	A	T	G	E	U	I	O	N	G
I	M	T	R	N	H	M	T	C	N	G
P	A	E	A	I	E	T	E	S	A	U
S	S	D	L	N	A	P	R	E	H	S
E	E	R	T	W	D	E	R	L	O	E
B	F	O	A	O	G	I	A	E	U	S
O	I	F	V	D	S	H	N	T	S	S
R	E	E	E	H	E	C	E	G	M	A
C	L	R	R	S	L	O	A	O	A	L
I	D	E	N	A	I	N	N	B	N	O
M	O	H	A	M	M	E	D	I	U	M

18

R	E	E	N	I	A	T	N	U	O	M
E	N	B	O	U	N	T	Y	O	U	B
A	P	E	T	D	O	O	U	R	A	N
R	A	E	P	N	I	R	D	O	D	O
E	L	C	M	A	L	E	I	U	E	S
G	L	H	A	M	L	E	T	E	L	N
N	I	G	H	T	I	N	G	A	L	E
A	D	I	T	A	L	C	U	M	L	H
V	A	E	U	K	A	Y	A	K	E	P
A	K	L	O	P	C	C	R	N	A	E
T	O	O	S	R	C	L	D	T	K	T
S	T	T	R	A	I	E	I	I	R	S
S	A	T	A	N	P	O	A	R	A	B
N	O	R	E	K	A	N	N	I	P	S

19

A	M	E	N	I	C	E	E	S	L	R
R	O	O	M	U	S	C	A	T	E	L
E	N	S	I	A	A	A	I	T	A	A
T	E	U	R	P	R	N	U	S	H	T
S	Y	C	A	M	O	R	E	I	U	E
E	R	R	G	O	N	U	O	H	R	M
H	A	I	E	R	G	F	B	W	O	A
C	N	C	A	M	E	R	O	O	N	G
N	A	K	T	O	O	I	A	E	T	G
A	C	E	A	N	R	G	R	P	N	O
M	D	T	T	S	G	A	T	A	E	T
R	A	E	N	O	I	T	N	N	V	H
O	C	L	A	O	A	E	L	G	O	A
N	E	L	C	N	P	H	T	A	E	M

20

C	A	S	K	E	T	C	H	T	G	H
A	Y	O	C	I	L	A	C	O	O	P
M	A	R	T	I	N	H	I	R	Y	O
P	I	T	T	L	E	T	N	R	A	P
E	C	N	T	N	D	O	U	A	I	L
C	S	O	O	E	E	B	M	P	I	A
I	A	R	P	A	R	V	P	R	S	R
R	Y	R	R	E	P	I	O	I	R	C
T	A	V	T	C	N	I	B	C	A	H
A	L	N	A	I	R	H	N	O	E	E
K	A	N	T	D	E	O	A	T	L	R
C	M	R	A	A	A	R	T	G	O	S
O	I	A	R	O	D	N	A	P	E	U
C	H	A	M	B	E	R	L	A	I	N

21

N	A	T	R	A	P	S	A	L	M	S
P	R	E	I	M	E	R	P	H	N	S
E	A	H	D	B	N	L	I	C	A	M
R	M	W	A	L	S	D	T	O	R	H
C	O	U	N	A	I	T	I	R	R	A
Y	M	O	S	C	O	W	R	R	A	R
P	I	N	K	K	N	E	K	O	R	B
R	N	E	Y	S	E	S	S	B	T	I
E	N	O	L	M	R	T	U	O	A	N
S	E	P	A	I	S	H	E	R	R	Y
S	S	E	R	T	C	A	H	E	A	R
C	O	O	K	H	A	M	P	E	R	A
O	T	N	O	R	O	T	R	I	A	S
T	A	Y	N	E	K	R	O	T	S	T

22

H	O	B	S	O	N	A	T	A	E	H
T	A	E	R	G	N	I	L	L	A	C
V	N	R	T	A	N	G	I	E	R	R
E	E	E	N	O	M	I	S	S	E	E
S	L	N	G	M	B	D	T	E	O	P
T	A	G	I	E	A	A	O	S	E	P
R	G	A	U	C	R	R	C	R	A	O
Y	R	R	E	B	E	L	K	C	U	H
B	L	I	O	H	E	I	T	A	O	C
R	R	A	E	I	N	N	O	B	O	O
E	R	F	T	S	I	G	N	I	C	I
D	A	Y	K	I	T	T	E	N	E	T
T	N	A	I	G	L	O	O	E	A	N
E	L	M	O	O	I	N	O	T	N	A

23

C	R	E	N	I	M	S	A	J	N	P
L	H	T	B	D	S	A	N	D	A	L
A	T	A	C	E	L	L	N	R	I	A
R	N	L	R	A	R	A	A	G	N	C
I	O	P	O	L	Y	G	O	N	O	K
N	M	K	M	A	O	U	J	N	D	E
E	D	A	W	N	S	T	R	E	E	T
T	T	R	E	B	O	R	T	M	L	G
U	O	R	L	B	N	O	T	E	A	H
N	I	R	L	R	N	P	B	S	C	A
L	V	I	P	E	R	R	O	R	A	N
A	E	H	T	E	E	T	O	O	C	A
W	H	P	O	N	D	L	O	H	I	O
K	C	O	C	D	O	O	W	E	A	R

24

T	I	O	R	T	E	D	S	L	I	K
N	O	I	N	U	I	E	O	E	A	O
E	G	N	O	P	S	C	U	I	C	R
L	S	V	U	I	U	N	T	K	C	E
I	K	C	O	L	M	E	H	E	E	A
T	O	N	I	L	A	I	U	Z	B	L
S	W	S	A	I	T	T	N	E	E	L
A	T	E	B	L	O	A	T	E	R	E
C	O	L	T	E	P	P	I	H	W	T
I	W	L	D	M	O	I	N	R	U	N
S	N	A	I	T	P	Y	G	E	E	A
S	M	H	A	V	P	E	D	L	A	R
E	C	A	N	N	I	P	O	L	E	A
J	O	N	A	T	H	A	N	E	T	T

25

A	S	E	E	S	I	R	A	H	P	R
G	E	R	B	I	L	M	M	A	A	E
U	I	A	P	B	E	I	A	Z	I	V
Y	R	U	B	Y	A	C	Z	L	P	L
Y	E	Q	P	L	T	A	O	I	A	I
K	P	S	A	S	H	H	N	T	L	S
C	P	A	R	S	E	E	O	T	M	K
U	A	L	L	E	R	E	D	N	I	C
T	S	E	I	H	J	N	O	T	S	A
N	B	H	A	C	A	I	O	E	T	R
E	N	N	M	L	C	R	M	R	R	R
K	O	P	E	C	K	A	G	I	Y	A
J	R	C	N	G	E	M	T	U	N	B
D	I	C	T	A	T	O	R	O	S	Y

26

B	A	K	E	R	C	D	E	V	O	N
C	A	R	L	E	O	N	H	N	G	O
S	N	L	A	T	N	A	I	I	N	I
N	E	C	I	R	C	L	E	N	I	L
A	S	R	L	I	R	R	R	D	D	L
P	R	A	E	E	E	E	M	I	L	A
D	E	N	B	V	T	V	B	A	O	D
R	D	A	O	E	E	E	W	N	G	E
A	N	S	P	R	I	N	G	A	A	M
G	A	E	O	T	R	R	I	N	Q	C
O	S	B	S	O	E	E	A	U	I	O
N	I	Y	C	N	W	V	E	H	G	K
N	O	I	T	C	A	E	R	E	N	E
Y	R	N	E	H	N	N	N	J	A	R

27

N	R	E	V	E	S	Y	L	H	E	D
C	O	L	L	E	E	N	I	G	E	R
O	N	N	N	L	T	T	A	I	R	A
W	G	I	R	O	C	N	H	E	E	C
I	O	A	T	S	O	A	A	L	A	I
R	B	R	O	S	L	S	P	A	L	R
R	P	G	R	O	U	S	E	R	L	E
A	A	A	T	A	M	A	R	G	I	L
L	P	A	O	R	B	U	F	R	N	A
P	Y	D	I	T	U	L	R	U	A	N
A	R	A	S	I	S	A	E	B	V	D
C	U	N	E	C	B	O	N	E	A	R
A	S	A	L	L	Y	K	C	A	H	E
N	I	C	H	E	A	T	H	R	O	W

28

D	L	A	N	O	R	M	A	N	D	Y
E	R	I	H	S	K	R	O	Y	R	R
Z	C	E	C	A	N	L	G	A	A	E
I	I	T	H	O	O	O	T	S	H	L
H	R	N	I	C	L	E	W	A	C	L
P	Y	E	C	O	R	R	T	D	R	A
L	L	I	H	C	R	U	H	C	O	G
E	P	T	E	S	O	O	L	V	S	N
D	Y	S	S	R	I	L	E	I	S	I
M	R	I	T	S	A	F	L	E	B	T
O	A	T	E	A	L	O	G	N	A	T
R	M	N	R	I	D	R	I	N	T	I
S	I	E	N	G	E	U	N	A	I	N
E	D	D	E	A	R	M	I	L	K	K

29

S	C	S	H	E	L	L	A	C	E	L
D	A	E	H	S	E	T	A	G	D	E
R	P	V	L	W	A	R	S	A	W	N
Y	T	E	N	I	N	C	I	A	I	O
E	A	N	R	A	A	A	S	E	N	L
R	I	I	T	S	C	H	E	R	Z	O
E	N	I	S	I	I	T	M	R	E	C
G	O	I	U	N	T	A	E	O	R	H
N	N	O	G	G	A	W	N	S	O	I
O	E	T	U	A	V	A	A	S	T	N
C	O	W	A	P	O	I	L	I	A	V
N	O	T	T	O	C	H	G	N	N	A
E	A	C	I	R	E	M	A	I	E	R
R	E	D	N	E	T	E	R	P	S	I

30

S	A	P	M	A	P	L	I	N	L	L
A	A	E	U	I	I	C	O	R	A	L
R	A	M	D	S	L	H	K	O	E	E
D	V	N	L	L	C	U	C	D	P	W
A	E	U	W	E	H	R	A	O	N	E
M	N	M	A	L	A	C	H	I	I	K
S	E	I	Y	H	R	H	A	I	F	A
O	G	S	C	A	D	W	C	F	P	B
N	O	M	A	D	I	A	I	I	U	E
O	R	A	A	E	E	R	T	E	M	R
S	D	T	T	S	E	D	I	V	A	D
L	Y	I	O	H	O	E	Z	I	P	E
I	H	S	S	O	O	N	E	L	O	E
W	E	T	H	E	R	S	N	O	W	N

31

L A R R A P A H C E R
E U I O K E I R L C O
M W F S E R G E A N T
A A I D A M A M B A C
C T D N A R B M E R E
N R I I S E A A N F R
O A E W R T R J S E I
N Z V W E S O D E S D
N U E I E E M N T V Y
E L L N D C E I O N O
L U A O N U T W N A J
J L R U I O E A A L N
L I O N E L R D I C A
P A M I R G L I P U B

32

R A M S A Y L L E K T
U O P T E N P E N C E
O H M S L E I G H I M
H E A A E E L A N T P
G C D T N O I N U R E
R T A A R K A N S A S
E O G N O C I G A P T
G R A V E S E N D P Y
O O S I I S E I D C S
R K C A R D S D N I O
Y M A D E I R A N R G
T A R U L N C E S A R
A I S C A A E R V L A
S S E T V Y R A N A C

33

A	H	C	T	O	C	S	P	T	O	E
L	S	T	H	A	T	E	H	R	H	T
T	A	U	R	U	S	I	S	A	L	A
O	B	S	U	O	E	E	T	P	K	G
N	O	I	S	I	V	E	L	E	T	O
N	T	C	H	I	E	A	P	Z	P	R
I	A	K	L	H	E	O	T	E	C	R
R	G	L	C	C	L	T	R	O	A	A
J	E	E	V	E	S	A	O	C	R	H
S	O	A	V	L	N	K	N	E	D	E
T	U	N	G	R	E	A	G	A	I	N
A	E	D	A	A	E	R	I	N	G	O
E	V	E	A	H	R	K	S	I	A	H
K	O	R	A	N	G	U	T	A	N	R

34

H	O	P	N	M	I	A	R	H	P	E
A	M	R	A	T	E	F	F	A	T	Y
N	A	I	H	T	O	L	R	R	L	T
N	V	V	K	T	I	A	M	R	F	R
A	E	A	A	A	S	G	A	O	E	A
S	R	T	R	I	D	E	R	W	T	E
O	I	E	T	G	R	O	O	I	I	H
H	C	E	S	A	I	L	O	R	S	T
A	K	S	A	R	B	E	N	L	H	U
D	P	L	A	N	K	T	O	N	B	O
R	A	O	R	E	C	T	N	I	A	M
I	S	O	G	T	A	U	R	U	R	N
A	H	P	O	T	L	C	E	R	O	O
N	A	Y	N	U	B	E	V	B	N	M

35

D	S	U	R	I	N	A	M	R	A	P
N	U	O	E	N	R	O	B	A	A	L
A	M	S	H	Y	L	R	T	L	T	U
L	M	R	T	T	I	A	E	E	O	M
G	E	O	A	I	A	S	R	G	R	B
N	R	T	E	N	T	E	D	O	U	B
E	C	A	L	I	B	A	N	R	C	U
W	U	R	N	R	O	C	N	U	R	L
G	R	E	A	T	B	S	O	I	A	L
U	Y	B	D	Z	B	U	T	O	C	D
I	T	I	A	H	Y	I	T	S	K	O
N	N	L	B	V	O	L	E	L	N	Z
E	R	C	A	P	A	U	L	E	E	E
A	C	I	A	M	A	J	F	K	L	R

36

T	F	A	R	C	R	E	V	O	H	C
P	R	N	P	M	M	V	I	A	A	R
E	A	A	Y	O	U	O	O	B	E	E
R	U	I	E	R	I	D	L	R	A	M
S	N	R	L	T	N	N	E	E	I	O
E	N	O	G	A	A	M	T	V	R	N
U	R	A	N	D	R	O	M	E	D	A
S	O	E	I	E	U	T	C	R	R	S
C	H	A	D	L	R	E	S	D	I	T
S	C	N	A	L	D	N	N	U	E	E
E	I	B	E	A	U	R	A	N	A	R
W	R	I	H	T	U	O	M	R	A	Y
O	E	A	B	I	R	C	H	I	L	E
C	J	O	H	N	S	O	N	S	I	B

37

T	N	A	S	A	E	P	R	I	S	M
E	O	R	E	G	O	N	A	N	E	A
P	R	G	T	L	C	O	N	A	D	H
A	T	O	I	A	A	U	K	N	A	T
R	A	M	M	B	L	I	O	C	N	A
A	M	L	O	Y	L	M	B	E	U	H
P	C	I	L	R	A	G	E	S	B	C
A	R	L	O	I	G	L	R	T	E	E
S	A	Y	D	N	H	A	C	O	C	N
S	W	E	L	T	A	C	N	R	A	O
O	F	N	A	H	N	I	N	T	R	T
V	I	K	I	N	G	E	I	I	O	S
E	S	R	R	A	E	R	D	N	H	A
R	H	O	D	Y	R	L	O	G	I	C

38

T	O	P	K	C	A	J	M	A	C	Y
O	Y	T	I	R	A	H	C	O	O	D
M	B	U	C	C	A	N	E	E	R	N
T	U	R	K	A	M	P	A	E	R	E
O	L	A	O	N	A	R	W	M	A	W
M	L	A	C	T	N	O	M	D	L	M
O	O	L	L	E	H	T	O	R	L	A
R	R	E	D	N	A	E	L	O	O	R
R	E	S	E	N	T	S	R	F	D	K
O	I	S	L	A	T	T	T	L	E	E
W	I	A	I	E	A	A	O	E	P	T
E	A	R	L	U	N	N	R	M	R	I
L	A	T	A	T	R	T	O	A	O	N
L	O	C	H	A	O	C	C	C	T	G

39

A	R	B	M	A	H	L	A	T	A	M
D	A	K	O	T	A	O	A	L	L	A
A	T	T	C	R	G	O	G	O	L	D
V	L	W	H	I	G	H	E	H	I	R
E	A	U	I	E	A	C	U	T	N	I
N	O	L	P	M	I	S	T	R	A	D
U	R	A	P	N	B	S	U	O	M	I
S	C	T	E	A	U	L	T	N	O	L
S	O	R	N	I	R	L	E	A	T	I
N	E	D	D	E	G	A	S	D	T	G
B	S	A	A	C	U	N	I	O	O	E
I	R	E	L	A	N	D	Y	S	O	N
T	U	N	E	R	D	A	R	N	O	C
E	N	E	R	G	Y	U	K	O	N	E

40

P	U	R	D	A	H	H	A	R	P	O
A	R	R	A	B	A	T	L	L	A	O
R	W	E	N	D	A	L	A	S	L	T
C	O	N	G	R	E	S	S	E	O	T
A	M	O	O	N	M	C	K	X	M	A
D	N	R	R	A	I	N	A	T	I	T
I	U	E	A	P	U	F	F	I	N	G
A	D	P	I	O	I	I	D	E	O	R
P	N	O	S	L	E	N	O	L	M	I
I	O	O	A	E	U	L	G	I	O	N
L	M	H	N	O	R	A	F	T	L	G
I	L	W	P	N	O	N	I	N	O	O
H	A	I	R	A	P	D	S	E	S	N
P	F	E	R	R	E	T	H	G	I	F

More Beaver Books

We hope you have enjoyed this Beaver Book. Here are some of the other titles:

Spy School A Beaver original. Everything the would-be spy needs to know: how to become a master of disguise, crack codes, shadow the enemy, and lots more, leading up to becoming a Master Spy! Top secret classified information written by Max Andersen and illustrated by David Mostyn

Beaver Crossword Book 8 A Beaver original. Eighty more crosswords from master-puzzler Pat Duncan: in this book the first word across in every puzzle starts with the letter G

Fantasy Tales A collection of strange and wonderful stories – some frightening, some fantastic – which make enthralling reading for people of ten and over. Edited by Barbara Ireson, author of a number of Beaver books including *Ghostly Laughter*

These and many other Beavers are available from your local bookshop or newsagent, or can be ordered direct from: Hamlyn Paperback Cash Sales, PO Box 11, Falmouth, Cornwall TR10 9EN. Send a cheque or postal order made payable to the Hamlyn Publishing Group, for the price of the book plus postage at the following rates:
UK: 40p for the first book, 18p for the second book, and 13p for each additional book ordered to a maximum charge of £1.49;
BFPO and Eire: 40p for the first book, 18p for the second book, plus 13p per copy for the next 7 books and thereafter 7p per book;
OVERSEAS: 60p for the first book and 18p for each extra book

New Beavers are published every month and if you would like the *Beaver Bulletin*, a newsletter which tells you about new books and gives a complete list of titles and prices, send a large stamped addressed envelope to:

Beaver Bulletin
The Hamlyn Group
Astronaut House
Feltham
Middlesex TW14 9AR

202976